Low Tax
Simple Tax
Flat Tax

Robert E. Hall

Alvin Rabushka

McGRAW-HILL BOOK COMPANY

New York   St. Louis   San Francisco
Hamburg   London   Mexico   Toronto

To

Christopher and Anne

Anton and Nyree

1 2 3 4 5 6 7 8 9 DOC DOC 8 7 6 5 4 3

ISBN 0-07-025669-1 {PBK}
       0-07-025670-5 {H.C.}

LIBRARY OF CONGRESS CATALOGING IN PUBLICATION DATA

Hall, Robert Ernest, 1943–
Low tax, simple tax, flat tax.
   1. Income tax—United States. I. Rabushka, Alvin.
II. Title.
HJ4652.H185 1983   336.24'15'0973   82-21655
ISBN 0-07-025669-1 [PBK]
ISBN 0-07-025670-5 [HC]

Book design by Roberta Rezk

Preface

To: The President of the United States
Members of the United States Congress

From: Robert E. Hall
Alvin Rabushka

Subject: The Simple Flat Tax

We urgently commend to your attention the need for immediate and thorough tax reform. The American people have lost their faith in the nation's tax system. The hideous complexity of the income tax is driving taxpayers to exasperation. Staggering resources go into preparing tax returns, checking and auditing them, making arrangements to minimize taxes through legal avoidance schemes, and into outright evasion of taxes. The costly effects of diminished incentives from the tax system are even larger. Heavy taxation first under the corporate tax and again under the personal tax diverts investment away from innovative new enterprises and into tax shelters.

We have an answer. Starting from the basic principles of sound taxation, we have designed a completely new tax system to replace the personal and corporate income taxes. Under our simple flat tax, all income would be taxed once and only once, at a uniform low rate of 19 percent. The system is not an academic abstraction. We have designed tax forms, rewritten the Internal Revenue Code, and worked out all the practical details of the simple flat tax. The new tax system has withstood the scrutiny of leading experts on taxation, and has been endorsed enthusiastically by many of them.

Our simple flat tax puts taxation onto a new philosophical basis. Today, the tax system puts tax rates of 50 to 70 percent on the most successful members of our society, but at the same time it lets many of them wriggle out of paying these heavy taxes. In the process, it seriously distorts their economic behavior. A minority among the successful who give in to heavy taxation face badly diminished incentives for further success. Others pursue shelters instead of productive effort. As a comprehensive remedy, our simple flat tax puts the same low tax rate on everybody's income above a standard personal allowance. At the outset, it collects somewhat less revenue from the successful and necessarily more from the average taxpayer. But as economic energies are redirected into productive activities in place of tax avoidance, the economy will grow more rapidly to a new higher level of income and well-being. By 1990, every income group will be unambiguously better off from the economic benefits of tax reform.

Although the idea of a flat tax has been around for some time, our plan is a fresh, carefully constructed step up from the current tax system. It works. It is fair, simple, and easy to understand. It increases incentives to work, save, and invest. It saves billions of dollars in paperwork. It lowers interest rates immediately. It balances the federal budget in a few short years. It creates new jobs and raises living standards. It supports the values of honesty and integrity of the American people.

Now, more than ever, the time is ripe for a simple flat tax. It enjoys grass-roots support from hundreds of organizations and millions of individuals. The flat tax brings together liberals, conservatives, and people of a hundred persuasions in between. Its supporters disagree with each other on many other subjects, but all believe in the benefits of a simple flat tax. For the first time, the forces behind the flat tax are strong enough to overcome the opposition of the special interests who are trying to preserve the unjustified tax breaks enjoyed by their members. Today, you have a real chance to replace the disgraceful income tax with a fair, simple flat tax. Don't lose that opportunity.

Contents

ACKNOWLEDGMENTS

Our colleague and friend, Milton Friedman, started the flat-tax movement more than thirty years ago, and we regard this book as an elaboration and extension of his idea. We are grateful for his criticism and suggestions.

A number of tax specialists have helped us refine our ideas at various stages in our work, including Laurence Kotlikoff, Lawrence Summers, David Bradford, Joseph Minarik, and Joseph Pechman. Almost twenty years ago, E. Cary Brown provided the theoretical foundations for our proposal in his graduate course in public finance, in which the first author was a student. None of these specialists endorses all the details of our proposal, and some of them disagree with its central features.

We are grateful to Senator Dennis DeConcini and to Senator Roger Jepson for providing opportunities to express our ideas to Congress, and to Robert Fiedler of Senator DeConcini's staff for extended comments and help.

Jonathan Cender provided outstanding research assistance in every aspect of our work. Ilse Dignam prepared the manuscript and she and Louise Sherman kept our offices functioning while we applied ourselves single-mindedly to writing. William Hammett and Joan Kennedy Taylor of the Manhattan Institute for Policy Research helped us find a publisher.

The Domestic Studies Program of the Hoover Institution supported every phase of our work, and we are grateful for the use of the Institution's outstanding facilities.

CHAPTER 1

Why the Income Tax
Has Failed

The U.S. economy is in terrible shape. Output has stagnated and unemployment threatens to linger indefinitely at 9 percent or higher. The stock market is at depression levels. Productivity is declining, an alarming reversal of its steady annual growth at 2 to 3 percent in earlier decades. Capital formation and saving are low and falling.

The federal tax system deserves an important part of the blame for this mess. Not only are Americans in revolt against their tax system, but the rebels largely agree about the proper form of a new tax system— it should put a low, flat tax on a comprehensive definition of income. Nothing less than a total overhaul of taxes is required. Incentives must be restored to the economy to promote both innovative new ideas and expansion of existing successes. Perverse subsidies in the tax system, which draw resources into unproductive uses, must be eliminated forth-with. A properly designed flat tax is just what we need to put the economy back on track.

Tax reform is a tough social issue. We will not conceal the prime obstacle—restoring incentives for the successful means giving up some of the revenue that we now get from taxing them heavily. The immediate impact of reform is to reduce taxes on the top earners and raise taxes on the average earner. Tax reform will pass by majority vote only if the average earner is persuaded, as we are, that restoration of incentives will revitalize the American economy.

Background

For as long as we can remember, every candidate for political office has railed against the federal income tax, depicting it as a disgrace to the human race. The complaints are many: that millionaires legally can pay no taxes whatsoever; that blue-collar workers cannot deduct the cost of a bologna sandwich while business executives write off the cost of a three-martini lunch; that the system is incomprehensible to all but a handful of tax lawyers and accountants; that it fosters cheating and outright noncompliance; that it drives honest, law-abiding Americans into the bowels of the underground economy; and that special interests benefit at the expense of the ordinary taxpayer.

Once elected, members of Congress regularly have turned their attention to these pressing issues of tax reform. Since 1954, they have refashioned the tax code nine separate times. And what has come from these reforms? Higher taxes, more forms, a bewildering variety of new exemptions, deductions, credits or exclusions, stories of yet more widespread evasion. A generation of broken promises to reform the tax system has left taxpayers demoralized and disappointed. Even the Internal Revenue Service says that its tax experts cannot agree on the proper amount of taxes due from any given household—from 1982, the IRS will no longer offer to fill out your tax returns on request, abandoning this earlier service to taxpayers.

All the while, the American economy has fallen into the doldrums. Compared with a robust 3 percent annual real growth rate between 1945 and 1973, which doubled living standards, the economy languishes in periodic recession, buffeted by high interest rates, high unemployment, depressed stock and bond markets, and falling real earnings for workers. Small wonder that many have sought relief through cheating on taxes or joining the underground economy. Let's try to put these trends in perspective and look at why they have given rise to the current broad based flat-rate tax reform movement.

Complexity

The income tax took effect in 1913 after three-fourths of the American states ratified the Sixteenth Amendment to the Constitution of the United States. In that first year, the personal income tax return, Form 1040, was two pages long and the accompanying instructions only filled two pages. Moreover, only four-tenths of one percent of the American population had to file a return. Easy enough. 1981 was another story. A complete Form 1040 booklet included 17 pages of the most frequently used schedules, and 44 pages of instructions to assist taxpayers in preparing their returns. The index to this hefty brochure contained 139 entries and the order blank on the inside rear cover listed 54 forms and instructional booklets that taxpayers could request by mail.

Ninety-three million returns, encompassing virtually the entire population, were filed in 1979. Over 55 million filed the standard Form 1040. For the 38 million who took advantage of the Short Form 1040A, it was still necessary to work through 10 pages of often bewildering instructions. Since the Internal Revenue Service estimates that college-level reading ability is required to obtain 90 percent comprehension of the instructions for preparing Form 1040A, it is not surprising that over 6 million taxpayers paid commercial firms to complete even this simplified return.

For 1972, as an example, the Government Accounting Office (GAO) reported that about 5 million people, who owed some $2 billion in income taxes, did not file returns. One-fourth completed 8 years or less of school. The GAO contended that many people with limited education may find the tax laws too complicated to complete and may even not be aware of their filing responsibilities. In short, trying to file a tax return, not to say anything about getting it right, was beyond the comprehension of more than one million persons.

Let's return to the personal income tax Form 1040, the most common document we all have to complete every year. Preparation of Form 1040 includes maintaining and reporting information of different sources of income, expenses, and deductions. It involves tedious and often confusing mathematical computations. Simply to see if one is eligible for a broad range of credits, exclusions, and deductions requires a thorough reading and comprehension of all of the instructions for several different tax forms. In 1975, for example, the Internal Revenue Service inventory included 293 principal tax forms and related schedules covering almost every aspect of financial activity. A typical filer of Form 1040 completes Schedule A to itemize his deductions, Schedule B to list dividends and interest receipts, Schedule C to report business income, Schedule D for capital gains and losses, and a host of other schedules for other forms of income, special credits, and the like. There are 38 instructions to add, subtract, or multiply on just the first two pages of the form plus Schedules A and B. The opportunities for error are enormous.

In processing over 90 million tax returns in 1979, the Commissioner of Internal Revenue estimated that computational errors on Form 1040 occurred on 7.3 percent of all returns. Although 3.8 million filers understated their income (an average of $241 per return), an astonishing 2 million overstated their income ($159 per return). Error rates on the Short Form 1040A, which only requires eight mathematical computations, exceeded 5 percent. To be absolutely clear, we are not talking about people who are caught trying to cheat. What we mean is that the tax forms are so complicated that it has become increasingly difficult just to calculate correctly taxes owed to the government.

Reflecting this complexity is the growth of commercial tax preparation. Thirty years ago, only 10 to 15 percent of the population sought professional help to complete their tax returns. By 1976, the figure reached 45 percent, and now exceeds 50 percent. Nor do these commercial organizations always get the right numbers in determining taxes owed. In its March 1976 issue, *Consumer Reports* cited a 1975 internal IRS survey which showed that people trained and employed by IRS computed the wrong tax 72 percent of the time handling relatively simple tax problems. A 1971 IRS survey of commercial tax-preparation firms disclosed an 82 percent error rate on low-income returns with itemized deductions. The only skilled group was certified public accountants, a very expensive source of help for the average taxpayer.

A few years ago, Ralph Nader's Tax Reform Research Group set out to test the IRS on its understanding of the income tax. They created a tax schedule for a fictional couple with one child and sent copies to 22 IRS offices throughout the country. Each office calculated a different tax liability, ranging from a high refund of $811.96 to a tax underpayment of $52.14.

The Internal Revenue Code of 1954, as amended, contains thousands of pages of tax regulation. It enumerates rules, exceptions to the rules, and exceptions to the exceptions. The complexity of the code has made it impossible to design a simple tax form and write clear, easy-to-follow instructions.

Some statistics on the tax code are mind-boggling. The entire Code of Federal Regulations, all general and permanent laws in force in the United States, has 50 different titles filling more than 180 volumes. Title 26, the Internal Revenue Code, is responsible for 14 of these volumes, of which 8 are just for the income tax. Title 26 occupies 14 inches of library shelf space. The eight volumes for the income tax fill 5,105 pages, cost $65.50 per set, and weigh 12 pounds 2 ounces. The 1981 Economic Recovery Tax Act amended some 89 separate sections in the tax code. To explain these changes, the staff of the Joint Committee on Taxation published a 411-page booklet. It takes more than a full-time job to keep abreast of changes in the law and regulations.

Lest you continue to doubt us at this point, next year try your hand at income averaging on Schedule G. Not only must you correctly fill out a current Form 1040, but you must also enter information from the four previous tax years. Then you must complete another set of calculations to determine if Schedule G means lower taxes than you would otherwise owe. The idea underlying income averaging is sound but its implementation is anything but simple.

We could write a book, as many have, on surviving the annual ordeal of tax preparation, or a book on the variety of ways that are available to reduce taxes legally. From all this it is easy to see why there is public clamor for true tax simplification that would condense the personal income tax return to a postcard.

Costs

How much does it cost Americans to prepare their annual income tax returns? We've all heard about the growing burden of federal reporting for individuals and businesses in complying with the information requirement of several dozen governmental agencies. The president's Office of Management and Budget has determined that federal tax forms alone comprise 78 percent of all federal reporting requirements. The Treasury Department estimated that the public spent 613 million hours in 1977 filling out some 260 different tax forms—about three hours for every man, woman, and child in the entire country. Here are the estimates of time spent completing 5 of the IRS forms:

Individual income tax return (1040)	148,960,000 hours
Wage and tax statements (W-2)	109,076,000 hours
Employers' quarterly federal tax return for employees (941)	86,984,000 hours
Recipient of interest and dividends (1099)	53,683,000 hours
Individual income tax return short form (1040A)	32,802,000 hours

A full picture of costs must add to the time spent filling out tax forms the costs of time and effort in assembling the mass of documents needed to support these returns: sales slips, receipts, accounting computer printouts, and other records accumulated and stored for many years by large numbers of taxpayers.

The business of commercial tax preparation has enjoyed rapid growth. In 1977, nearly half of all taxpayers used tax preparers and paid over $1 billion to commercial firms, or about $27 per return. If we attach a similar price to the effort of those who filled out their own forms, the direct dollar value of tax preparation would have amounted to $2.3 billion that year.

To these direct costs we should add the cost of maintaining necessary tax records on the assumption that at least as much effort is involved in record-keeping as in reading and understanding the instructions and filling out the tax form itself. For 1977, then, the $2.3 billion figure doubles to at least $4.6 billion. Higher prices since 1977 put an estimate for 1982 in the $8 billion neighborhood.

Apart from these direct costs, taxpayers must also support the operations of the Internal Revenue Service. Its budget, too, has steadily grown from about $2 billion in 1978 to nearly $3 billion for 1983. About one-third of this is spent processing returns and providing taxpayer service. Another third is budgeted for examinations and appeals. A truly simplified income tax might allow us to reduce the IRS budget by about one-half. As people were sure that all taxpayers paid their lawfully fair share, less could be spent on investigations and collections as well. At present about one-third of the IRS budget goes just for checking and processing the hundreds of numbers that are reported and entered into a typical tax return.

To summarize, taxpayers bear some $9 to $10 billion in real costs for preparing and verifying their taxes, above and beyond what they actually pay in taxes!

Direct costs to taxpayers of $8 billion, with indirect costs of a billion or so supporting the activities of the Internal Revenue Service, are only the tip of the iceberg. Taxpayers invest literally a fortune in time and effort to rearrange their activities so as to reduce the amount of taxes they have to pay each year. In the 50 percent bracket, an extra dollar of earnings nets the earner only 50 cents after tax. On the other hand, a dollar saved in taxes is worth a dollar—twice as much as a dollar earned. So we should not be surprised that tax avoidance—the more pleasant euphemism is tax shelters—is a commonplace activity or topic for discussion in every middle-class American household. Tax avoidance, the exploitation of loopholes in the law to reduce taxes, has grown to the hundred-billion dollar level. Tax evasion, the deliberate effort to hide or underreport income, has also grown to the hundred-billion dollar level, making the underground economy a subject of growing academic study. The dead-weight loss to the economy from all of this effort to reduce or escape taxation has been estimated at $50 billion or more, which would otherwise find its way into productive use. $50 billion is equal to $250 for every American, or $1,000 for a typical family of four.

The Graduated Tax Rate Schedule

Tax avoidance and evasion owe much to the existence of a steeply graduated federal income tax system in which marginal tax rates rise from a low of 14 percent to a high of 50 percent. (The marginal rate is the amount by which the tax goes up for each additional dollar of income. For married couples filing jointly in 1982, the first $3,400 of taxable income is not taxed. Each dollar of taxable income between $3,400 and $5,500 is taxed at a fixed rate of 12 percent. From $5,500 to $7,600, the rate is 14 percent. The next $4,300 is taxed at 16 percent, and so on up to amounts over $85,600, which are taxed at 50 percent.) Despite a statutory maximum of 50 percent for the personal income tax, a reduction in 1982 from the previous higher 70 percent rate, real rates run much higher for dividend and interest income. Corporations must first pay a 46 percent tax rate on profits. Dividends paid to individuals from these profits are again taxed at rates up to 50 percent, which means that real tax rates on dividend income exceed 70 percent.

To see why high marginal tax rates foster tax avoidance and evasion requires a clear understanding of the difference between the notions of one's average tax rate or burden and one's marginal tax rate. The tax burden of each taxpayer is the share of his income that he pays to the government in taxes. So a family that pays $5,000 in taxes from an income of $50,000 has an average tax of 10 percent.

Marginal tax rates apply only to the last dollar earned. As increases in income push people into higher tax brackets, a greater proportion of each additional dollar of income is paid in taxes. Someone paying a marginal rate of 20 percent gets to keep 80 cents of each additional dollar. At 30 percent, he keeps 70 cents. And at a 50 percent marginal rate, he divides the last dollar equally between himself and the government. Many families today have incomes of $50,000, pay an average tax of $5,000 (or 10 percent), yet face marginal rates from 30 to 50 percent. It is this top marginal rate, not the average rate, that sets incentives. The marginal rate determines whether the taxpayer decides to work harder or spend more time fishing.

Twenty years ago, few Americans paid high marginal tax rates on their income. Today, millions of middle-class Americans face high marginal rates that were intended only for the very rich just a short while ago. The dramatic increase in marginal tax rates has been most serious for the upper-middle part of the income spectrum. A professional or executive earning $50,000 in 1979 faced a 43 percent marginal tax rate if he or she was married and had a non-earning spouse; in 1965, the same individual with the same salary, adjusted for inflation, paid a marginal tax rate of only 25 percent. We should not think that high marginal tax rates are a clever device whereby the middle class soak the rich in supporting the activities of government. It may be instructive at this point to review the history of the federal income tax to understand why tax avoidance and evasion are so popular, threatening the very foundation of the federal revenue system.

Americans got their first taste of the income tax in 1913. The income tax law of that year granted a personal exemption of $3,000 for a single person and $4,000 for married persons. The basic tax rate started at one percent. In addition to the normal rate of one percent, a surtax was levied on the net incomes of individuals exceeding $20,000 at a rate of one percent. The rate of this surtax rose in stages to 6 percent on incomes over $500,000, capping the richest of Americans with a top marginal rate of 7 percent. Only four-tenths of one percent of the population filed a tax return in 1913. Corporate profits were also taxed at a normal rate of one percent without provision for a surtax. To put this tax in perspective, all federal tax receipts in 1913 only amounted to 2.6 percent of the Gross National Product.

During congressional debate on the Sixteenth Amendment, proponents of the income tax promised that the top rate could never conceivably surpass 10 percent. World War I quickly gave the lie to these promises. Wartime needs for revenue reduced the personal allowance, imposed a normal rate beginning at 4 percent, and raised the surtax up to 50 percent for those with incomes over $1 million. Still, only about one-fifth of the adult population filed income tax returns.

Secretary of the Treasury Andrew Mellon reduced the structure sharply during the 1920s, bringing the top marginal rate down to 25 percent. But the depression and war years of the 1930s and 1940s pushed the top rates back above 50 percent. Indeed, the top marginal rate stood at the incredible level of 91 percent when President John F. Kennedy proposed in 1963 to reduce the top rate to 70 percent. President Reagan's 1981 Economic Recovery Tax Act further lowered the top marginal rate to 50 percent.

According to Treasury Department figures, a family of four earning the median income in 1965 faced a marginal rate of income tax of 17 percent. In 1980, its marginal rate was 24 percent. For families with twice the median income, the marginal rate increased from 22 to 43 percent. If a family's income only kept pace with inflation during this period, the purchasing power of its take-home pay would have declined as the family paid taxes at increasingly higher rates, leaving it with a smaller share. As this process accelerated during the high inflation years of the late 1970s, taxpayers faced a growing squeeze on real take-home pay.

During 1982, families earning $20,000 paid marginal rates of 28 percent. Those earning $40,000 paid marginal rates of 44 percent. By 1982, ordinary middle-income households paid high marginal tax rates conceived originally only for millionaires, and then when the dollar was really worth a dollar.

Since 1913, federal receipts have risen from 2.6 percent of GNP to more than 20, an eightfold increase in the share of our national income going to federal taxes. The income tax is a direct culprit of this growth, providing 48 percent of all government revenue. More than 90 million households and single persons currently file tax returns. Those critical of increasing federal spending can impose a guilty verdict on the federal income tax.

Who pays the federal income tax? In 1980, the Tax Foundation reported that the highest 10 percent of taxpayers paid 51.8 percent of all federal income taxes, up from 48.6 percent in 1975. The highest 25 percent—one-fourth of all taxpayers—paid 77.5 percent. The bottom half, in comparison, paid only 6 percent of all federal income taxes.

Return to the upper quarter. In 1980, this quartile included all households with incomes of $21,425 or higher. For this one-fourth of the American population that pays more than three-fourths of all income taxes, marginal tax rates range from 30 to 50 percent. It is easy to see why they pay so much attention to sheltering income from taxation, a legal form of tax reduction, or to engaging in underground or black-market economic activities, an illegal form of tax reduction.

Tax Evasion

A flood of books and articles have appeared in the past few years trying to determine the causes and size of the underground economy. The underground economy is made up of more than prostitutes, drug merchants, and gamblers. It includes millions of otherwise respectable people—doctors, lawyers, accountants, carpenters, plumbers, contractors, retailers, restaurateurs, and others—who engage in legal activities but fail to report all or some of their income to avoid paying taxes. The income generated in the underground economy does not appear in the GNP totals. Estimates of the size of the underground economy range to the several hundred-billion dollar level.

Other people simply underreport their income, a deliberate effort to cheat on taxes. Tax evasion—noncompliance with the tax code—has reached staggering proportions. IRS estimates that tax evasion in 1973 cost the United States Treasury $29.3 billion, a figure that tripled to $87.2 billion by 1981. IRS projects a rise in outright tax evasion to the $120 billion level by 1985. Nor do these sums include unreported income from drugs, prostitution, and gambling, which represents another $9.8 billion lost in taxes in 1981.

How important is tax evasion? The federal government ran a budget deficit of $100 billion in fiscal year 1982. If taxpayers fulfilled their lawful obligation, the budget deficit would virtually have disappeared. To the extent that budget deficits cause high interest rates, greater compliance would help relieve that problem. Many are even concerned that unchecked growing evasion threatens the self assessment foundation of the American income tax system. In our system, individuals bear responsibility for reporting all their income, calculating the correct amount of taxes, and sending in payment. Failure to file, report all income, or pay taxes lowers Treasury receipts, widens the budget deficit, and threatens national solvency.

The largest amount of unreported income from legal sources comes from self-employment activities, followed by wages, interest payments, and rents and royalties. Since the Internal Revenue Service audits less than 2 percent of all tax returns—the percentage fell from 3.39 percent in 1965 to 1.58 percent in 1982—few risk getting caught. The problem of tax evasion from unreported income had grown so large that the IRS designated a study team in the spring of 1978 to evaluate its scope. Using available 1976 statistics, the team concluded that unreported income from self-employment ran to 40 percent of the amount which should have been declared on the tax return. Unreported income from interest ran to 16 percent, from dividends 16 percent, from rents and royalties 50 percent, from capital gains 22 percent. The only airtight source of compliance was in wages and salaries, with underreporting at less than 2 percent. Thus a large part of nonsalaried income escapes the IRS tax net. Most of this income is received by middle- and upper-income households.

Even those taxes that are not evaded are not always paid. The IRS says that it is owed $20.5 billion in back taxes waiting to be collected. In the same breath, IRS gives the opportunity to pay in installments whether or not taxpayers can afford to pay back taxes in one lump sum.

To be fair, high marginal tax rates are not the sole cause either of the underground economy or just plain cheating on taxes. Some say the underground economy is partly countercyclical—the recession drives laid-off workers into the underground economy. As well, Americans have a growing distrust of government to accompany their dislike of higher taxes. But rising noncompliance is a direct response to the higher taxes people are paying as they are pushed by inflation into higher tax brackets.

Cheating on taxes, like the budget deficit, has become a hundred-billion dollar enterprise. Accompanying evasion is a corresponding rise in tax avoidance, which threatens to become an equally gigantic national enterprise. Many of our most prominent citizens, including past presidents, cabinet officers, corporate presidents, religious and community leaders, have received unwanted notoriety from declaring on their returns a sometimes shady deduction or loss that serves to shelter income from taxes.

Tax Avoidance

The Internal Revenue Code proclaims its intent to tax all income from whatever source derived. But Congress has riddled it with some 500 exclusions, exemptions, deductions, and credits, commonly called loopholes. So extensive are these loopholes that the nation's total AGI (adjusted gross income, the number on the bottom line of the first page of Form 1040) is only about 70 percent of all personal income. Further deductions lower taxable income, the third line on page 2, to about half of personal income. Somewhere in the neighborhood of half of all personal income escapes federal income taxation.

The best way to understand why so much income escapes taxation is to dig out last year's Form 1040 and leaf through its various schedules. On the bottom of the first page is a section called "Adjustments to Income." Payments to a retirement plan—an Individual Retirement Account or a self-employed Keogh plan—are a way to shelter income. You may reduce your adjusted gross income for tax purposes by the amount of your retirement contribution. Someone in the 50 percent tax bracket who contributes $10,000 to a Keogh plan thereby reduces his taxes by $5,000. The amount of tax you would save depends on your marginal rate: the lower your marginal rate, the fewer tax dollars saved, and vice versa.

Another entry in this category is alimony. Alimony is a good example of a general problem we will call leakage. Alimony usually goes from the former spouse with the higher income to the one with the lower income, which also means that it goes from the one with the higher marginal tax rate to the one with the lower rate. The government comes out behind when one person deducts alimony and the other declares it as income. Few people deliberately divorce their spouses to pay alimony payments for the sole purpose of writing off such payments from their adjusted gross income, but the tax treatment of alimony still creates a tax shelter.

Leaf ahead to Schedule A, the page for listing itemized deductions. In the first section we can deduct medical and dental expenses in excess of 3 percent of our adjusted gross income from AGI. Medical deductions are a major source of abuse of the opportunity to itemize deductions—people have gotten away with deducting fancy swimming pools by claiming them as medically justified.

Move to the bottom of the left-hand column, to the category "interest expense." Interest paid on borrowed money is the single largest vehicle used to shelter income. In 1979, interest expense came to $74.4 billion. Of that sum, $48.5 billion was due to home mortgage interest, which makes owner-occupied housing the single biggest tax shelter in the United States. The inflationary run-up in housing prices in the 1970s owes much to the tax deductibility of mortgage interest, which grew increasingly valuable as more and more taxpayers were pushed into higher tax brackets and inflation raised interest rates. Remember, the value of any deduction is determined by your marginal rate, so that a poor or lower-middle income wage earner, who is in a lower tax bracket, benefits less from a deduction than a wealthier taxpayer, who is in a higher bracket.

But the rate code does not discriminate solely in favor of owner-occupied housing. All interest expenses are deductible. Many exotic tax shelters are constructed largely on the deductibility of borrowed money, enabling the taxpayer to write off all interest costs against current income, which may be taxed at a 50 percent rate. Any profits from the sale of the property in the future would only be subject to the much lower capital gains rate of 20 percent.

Scanning the pages of *The Wall Street Journal* and other financial magazines reveals a shopping basket full of oil, gas, cattle shelters, properties, and seminars at which experts will explain ways to shelter your income lawfully from taxation. Here is how a typical shelter works: You buy a share of an oil drilling partnership. A bank lends the partnership two or three times what the partners have put in. The drilling costs of the partnership are fully deductible business expenses, along with the interest paid to the bank. You get three or four dollars of deductions for each dollar you invest. If you are in the 50 percent tax bracket, the deductions put you ahead by $1.50 or $2.00 for each dollar you have invested.

The U.S. tax law is full of gimmicks for special interest groups and for particular social effects. Special Analysis G of the Budget of the United States Government lists all items in the tax code that qualify for tax subsidies. A tax subsidy item is one that receives a special break resulting in its being taxed at less than the normal highest rate. The list includes items in classification that range from national defense to the environment to housing, health, transportation, income security, and veterans' benefits. Table G-2 in the volume contains 95 separate classifications. Estimates of revenue loss range from a low of $5 million, for exclusion of interest on local government industrial development bonds for mass transit, to a high of $25.5 billion for home mortgage interest. With high marginal tax rates facing the entire middle class, the lure to shelter income is almost irresistible.

The Internal Revenue Service publication *Statistics of Income* for 1979, the most recent year for which data are available, shows that the total adjusted gross income for the 26.5 million Americans who itemized their deductions was $796 billion. In all, these taxpayers itemized $184 billion in deductions, reducing AGI by 23 percent to taxable income of $612 billion. These numbers will doubtless run higher in 1982. It would not be unreasonable to conjecture a ball-park estimate of tax shelters in the region of $100 billion and steadily rising.

To repeat, tax avoidance is not illegal. The tax code specifically authorizes taxpayers to take advantage of every lawful exclusion or deduction. But when people arrange their financial affairs largely to shelter income from taxation, instead of producing more income for taxation, the economy as a whole suffers and the Treasury collects fewer tax receipts.

Tax evasion and tax avoidance point up two dimensions of a general concept we affectionately call leakage. Leakage shrinks the potential tax base by at least a quarter, which means the remaining three-quarters must be fixed at higher rates to meet the government's budgetary requirement.

Leakage

Leakage refers to all the different ways, mainly legal but also illegal, that national income escapes taxation. Some types of leakage are readily measured because they are included in GNP; others are a matter of conjecture because they come from the unrecorded activity in the underground economy. Income that leaks away from taxation includes:

> Types of corporate and individual income on which the Internal Revenue Code does not require reporting: Fringe benefits make up by far the bulk quantitatively.

> Adjustments to income that result in lower Adjusted Gross Income for individuals: In addition to small items like employee moving expenses that appear on the 1040, these include large deductions made on partnership returns where only the bottom line after deductions appears on the 1040.

> Deductions that further reduce Adjusted Gross Income to a smaller Taxable Income: These include interest, medical expenses, state and local taxes, and charitable contributions.

> Unreported income from interest, dividends, professional activity, and the like.

Gross National Product is the most comprehensive measure of income available for the United States. In 1979, the last year for which we have detailed tabulations of tax returns, GNP was $2414 billion. The Adjusted Gross Income of individuals in the same year was only $1465 billion, just 61 percent of GNP. Almost 40 percent of GNP leaks away before it is taxed. The three biggest sources of leakage at this stage are untaxed fringe benefits paid to workers, excise and property taxes paid by businesses, and depreciation deductions.

More leakage occurs between AGI and the incomes actually taxed by the income tax. All taxpayers are permitted to deduct the ''zero bracket amount''; this totaled $231 billion in 1979. Some taxpayers itemize deductions above the zero bracket amount, to the tune of $101 billion. Taxpayers were allowed exemptions for themselves and dependents amounting to $225 billion in 1979. What is left after these many steps is an extraordinarily small fraction of GNP. The remainder is so small that high tax rates need to be applied to it in order to generate enough revenue for the federal government.

We should be clear at this stage that not all forms of leakage are necessarily bad—we do not favor a tax that is a straight percentage of GNP. Depreciation deductions, for example, are in the tax system to provide incentives to invest, and simply removing them would be harmful to capital formation. Personal exemptions, the zero bracket amount, and other devices to limit the taxation of the poor are also desirable. A well-designed tax system will have a straightforward provision for investment incentives and a simple personal allowance, but otherwise will tax all of GNP.

The interplay between leakage and tax rates is revealing. Total receipts from the personal and corporate income taxes were $280 billion, amounting to 11.6 percent of GNP. Thus a straight tax of 11.6 percent on all gross income would yield the same revenue as the 1979 system of taxing corporate profits at 46 percent and an individual's "taxable income" at rates from 14 to 70 percent. The reason for the huge disparity between the hypothetical 11.6 percent flat rate and the high corporate and individual rates is the erosion of the Gross National Product into a very much smaller taxable base of income. Subtracting from GNP such items as fringes, indirect business taxes, unreported income, and itemized deductions shrinks the tax base by half. To raise the same 11.6 percent of GNP in revenue from this contracted base requires much higher rates. The only way to lower rates is to broaden the tax base. Again, we do not advocate the straight tax on GNP, but rather a simple tax with a broad base, reduced from GNP only by investment incentives and personal allowances.

One of the most critical sources of leakage in the current tax system is its treatment of interest. Fixing up the devastating problems of interest taxation and deduction is one of the major ingredients of our simple flat-tax proposal in Chapter 3. Current tax principles rest on the notion that interest receipts are part of income and interest payments are, logically enough, negative income, or deductions. But taxpayers are tremendously clever at taking the deductions against income taxed at high rates, where the deductions are most valuable, and reporting the income in ways that are taxed at low rates, or not taxed at all. Though the total volume of leakage from interest deductions is not large compared to the big items—especially untaxed fringe benefits— many important economic inefficiencies stem from interest leakage, which makes this subject worth elaborating.

According to the National Income Accounts of the U.S. for 1979, the total interest earnings of the American public were $210 billion. This counts only the amount paid by businesses and the government to individuals, and not any interest paid by one individual to another. On the other hand, interest paid by consumers to businesses was $44 billion. On net, individuals received some $166 billion in interest. But their income tax returns, when added together, tell an entirely different story. Reported interest income was only $74 billion. Even worse, total interest deductions were also $74 billion. Their tax returns don't confess to any net interest receipts at all, though the national income accounts report $166 billion.

Taxpayers use all kinds of tricks, some legal and some not, to distort their interest income and deductions. Pension funds are an important contributor. These funds hold bonds on behalf of taxpayers, but the taxpayers are not required to report the interest earned by the funds until the pension is actually paid. Clever taxpayers in high brackets set up interest transactions with their children with the effect that the parents get deductions at their high tax rates while the children get interest income which may not have to be reported at all. These transactions need not have any economic substance. You can give your son $10,000, borrow it back at 12 percent interest, take the interest deduction on $1200 per year, and use that interest, as your son's custodian, for sending him to a summer camp you would have paid for anyway. The net effect is nothing more than to give you a $1200 interest deduction, worth $600 in reduced taxes if you are in the 50 percent bracket.

A distressing number of taxpayers use an even simpler technique for saving the taxes on interest—they leave their interest income off their returns. According to the IRS study of unreported income, 16 percent of interest income is unlawfully omitted from people's tax returns.

Supply-Side Economics and Tax Reduction

Supply-side economics, with its emphasis on expanding investment, savings, work effort, and output, has put its mark on U.S. tax policy in recent years. Supply-siders stress incentives. They focus on reducing marginal tax rates to get people to work harder and save more. With the general rise in taxes and the particular rise in high marginal rates, we have increasingly taxed work, savings, and investment, getting less of all three. At the same time, we have subsidized leisure, borrowing, and consumption, getting more of all three. Supply-siders partly blame high marginal tax rates for the poor performance of the economy characterized by declining savings, high unemployment, low rates of capital formation, and severely distressed stock and bond markets. The supply-sider firmly believes that a tax system with low marginal rates is the key to stimulating high rates of economic growth.

President Reagan entered office with a good deal of fanfare, heralding the new age of supply-side economics. His proposed plan for across-the-board reductions in tax rates would increase the incentives for Americans to work, save, and invest. The economic bonanza that must follow would also permit him to increase defense spending and balance the budget by 1984. Enactment of his 1981 Economic Recovery Tax Act put in place a three-year phased-in personal income tax cut, accelerated depreciation for business, and a variety of savings incentives.

The economy failed to respond in 1981. It also failed in 1982. Critics of Reaganomics blame the president's massive tax cut for burgeoning federal deficits which in turn, they claim, keep interest rates at record high levels. Other critics point to the failure of the Federal Reserve Board to pursue a steady monetary policy. Still others say the recession of 1981–82 was inherited from President Carter. This debate will doubtless continue for years to come.

Supply-side economics may become discredited from the performance of the economy in the first two years of the Reagan administration. But it is important to understand that President Reagan's tax reductions were not a real test of supply-side economics.

The president originally proposed the Kemp-Roth plan, a 30 percent across-the-board reduction in tax rates to take effect on January 1, 1981. Instead, after much political wrangling, he settled for a 25 percent reduction: 5 percent effective October 1, 1981, with additional 10 percent cuts on July 1, 1982, and July 1, 1983. However, these statutory tax-rate cuts are more ephemeral than real.

Almost as quickly as taxpayers benefit from legislated rate reductions in income taxes, they are pushed into higher tax brackets as a result of inflation or increases in real income, a phenomenon known as "bracket creep." Thus taxpayers face higher marginal rates, and pay a higher share of their income in taxes, because the increase in income is taxed at a higher rate. Inflation simultaneously erodes the purchasing power of all remaining take-home dollars. The net effect is that real purchasing power may not increase—or may even decline—despite an apparent increase in salary that keeps pace with inflation. Congress's

Joint Committee on Taxation estimated that bracket-creep-induced tax increases in 1981 would offset 86 percent of the dollar value of tax relief contained in the original Kemp-Roth plan, 72 percent in 1982, and 68 percent in 1983. Because the tax cut was postponed and reduced, bracket creep makes the effective tax cut smaller still. Rising social security taxes, along with increased state and local government taxes in 1981 and 1982, offset what was left. Professor Richard McKenzie showed in a *Wall Street Journal* article that typical families with a low income of $15,000, a median income of $24,000, and a high income of $45,000 will all have higher average tax rates and lower after-tax purchasing power in 1984 than in 1980. The average tax will rise from 17.8 to 19.4 percent for the low-income family; for the median-income family, from 24.5 to 25.1 percent; and for the high-income family, from 33 to 34.6 percent. From this point of view, President Reagan's "tax cuts" only moderated an otherwise even sharper rise in taxes. This is not the stuff of supply-side tax cuts.

In August 1982, President Reagan signed a tax hike measure totaling $99 billion over the next three years. While not eliminating or reducing the final 10 percent phase of the three-year, 25 percent rate reduction, the measure signals a mild retreat from the fundamental thesis of incentive-restoring tax cuts.

Those who seek a real supply-side tax cut have pinned their banners to the flat-tax bandwagon. The flat-rate tax promises a top marginal rate below 20 percent, which would also balance the federal budget at current spending levels. It would end bracket creep, marriage penalties, penalties for success, curtail the attractiveness of the underground economy, reduce the 50-cent subsidy in a tax shelter for someone now in the 50 percent bracket to only 20 cents, and eliminate a myriad of economic distortions in the tax code.

Although we respect the arguments of the supply-siders, our claims for the economic benefits of a fundamental improvement in incentives from the simple flat tax are much more cautious. We foresee a gradual improvement of the economy for a whole decade after enactment of tax reform, cumulating to an increase in real incomes of perhaps 9 percent. Chapter 5 lays out our views on how this process will proceed.

In the next chapter we look at the flat tax philosophy and the grassroots movement which has sprung up behind it.

CHAPTER 2

The Flat Tax Movement

The idea of a flat-rate tax is not a new discovery. Milton Friedman, for example, proposed it in his 1962 book *Capitalism and Freedom*. As a serious, viable policy, however, the idea burst onto the national scene in 1982. By summer it had become the single most talked-about subject in Washington, D.C., resulting in congresssional hearings in July with promises of further hearings to come after Labor Day. How and why did this transformation come about?

The starting point is December 10, 1981, when we first published in *The Wall Street Journal* our proposal to replace the current federal tax system with a flat tax. The centerpiece of that article was a proposed simple tax form that would fit on a postcard. The article generated a spate of calls and correspondence, some of which were reprinted in the *Journal*'s letters section. A surprising number of letters came from lawyers and accountants who felt that despite a potential loss of personal business, a low, flat-rate tax was a great improvement over the present system.

From late January, after IRS mailed out the Form 1040 tax forms, until April 15, the deadline for filing, interest in the flat tax continued to grow. We expected the public to shift its attention to other issues on April 16. This did not happen. Editorial endorsements in *The New York Times*, the *Washington Post*, and the *Christian Science Monitor*, among others, spurred an even more rapid growth of interest in the flat tax. Between February and June, members of Congress introduced nearly a dozen flat-tax bills. Stories appeared in nearly every major daily newspaper, weekly magazine, and financial journal; syndicated columnists and the national networks debated its pros and cons. It was raised during a presidential press conference in June, catching Mr. Reagan by surprise. In July he felt compelled to instruct his chief-of-staff, James Baker, to undertake a review of the subject. Budget director David Stockman said the president might propose a flat tax in his 1984 budget message.

By summer, spokesmen for special interests began to speak out against eliminating the deductibility of home mortgage interest and charitable contributions, among others. Some critics said that a flat tax was just a ruse to cut taxes for the rich and increase taxes on lower- and middle-income families. Until early summer the flat tax was only an interesting idea. By late summer, when opposition publicly surfaced, the flat-tax had become a serious idea. By fall, the ideas had become concrete proposals for legislation.

From the typewriters of two Stanford professors to a national grass-roots movement, the proposal for a flat tax tapped a responsive chord in the public. On the one hand, the philosophy underlying a simple, low flat-rate tax repudiates the complexity and burdensome costs imposed on taxpayers as individuals and on the economy as a whole in filling out forms and trying to minimize taxes. It also terminates practices that allow millionaires to escape income taxes legally, and that punish success by imposing high tax rates on middle- and upper-income families. The flat tax is a protest against the dishonesty and cheating that has infected millions of otherwise law-abiding Americans, and turned the rest of us into seekers of tax shelters. In a positive vein, the flat-tax movement is a reassertion of fundamental American values, reflecting the American commitment to honesty, fairness, hard work, savings, investment, and success. Most Americans do not begrudge paying a reasonable share of their income in taxes to support government services. But they resent the current tax system, which distorts or subverts all of those enduring values.

A National, Grass-Roots Movement

No organized constituency conceived and masterminded the development of the flat-tax movement. Senator Dennis DeConcini of Arizona, a Democrat, introduced one of the first bills (S. 2147) on March 1, 1982, after extensive consultation with us—the bill is, in effect, the plan we outline in Chapter 3. Republican Representative Phil Crane of Illinois had earlier introduced a flat-tax bill in February. On April 5, Democratic Representative Leon Panetta of California introduced his bill, which closely resembles parts of the Hall-Rabushka proposal. The flat tax is not a Republican idea in origin or spirit. Indeed, President Reagan's first public reaction to the flat tax took the form of wondering out loud whether contributions to charities and other cultural organizations might decline from the loss of tax deductibility. Although Citizens Voice, an arm of the U.S. Chamber of Commerce, and the National Taxpayers Union, among others, have publicly endorsed the idea, each of these groups only joined a growing bandwagon already in progress that brought together under one conceptual umbrella a diverse, often conflicting community of social, economic, and political interests.

The Flat-Tax Coalition

The flat-tax movement spans the political spectrum, encompassing the conservative right, moderate Republicans, the bulk of the nonpartisan independent center, liberal Democrats, and even the radical left. It includes a religious appeal to honesty. It enjoys the support of supply-siders, orthodox balanced-budget fiscal conservatives, and liberal Keynesian economists. Many syndicated columnists have examined the concept. Such a coalition makes strange bedfellows indeed. For the same reason, opponents of the flat tax will find it hard to derail or halt the movement with a single, well-placed charge. Why does the movement enjoy such broad-based support?

The flat tax appeals to the liberal left. Liberals strongly believe in a progressive tax system, which for them means that rich people should pay a higher share of their income in taxes than poor people. To attain this goal, they have endorsed the graduated rate structure of the present income tax, which taxes higher-income households at successively steeper rates. However, they are unhappy with the hundreds of loopholes Congress has inserted into the tax code that allow some very rich people to pay little or nothing in taxes. The progressive rates in the statute are at odds with reality. Liberals, who believe in an extensive role for government, have a second concern. They fear that the rise of the underground economy and the tax cheating that high rates promote may reduce the flow of revenue to Washington, D.C., and jeopardize the raft of government programs they have built over the past few decades.

The flat tax can thus better serve the cause of liberals than the current system. It would eliminate all loopholes in the form of deductions, exclusions, and credits, insuring that all millionaires pay at least a fixed percentage of their income in taxes, say, 19 percent. The poor and middle-income would be sure that the rich could not buy expensive legal advice to escape taxes. Also, a flat-rate tax is progressive when a personal allowance for adults and dependents is granted, thus exempting the poorest from any income tax and insuring that lower-middle income households would pay a smaller share of their income in taxes than wealthier households. A flat tax would discourage underground economic activity, cheating, and shelters. It could provide more, not less, revenue to sustain government spending on social programs.

The flat tax appeals to the conservative right. Those who believe in a free-market economy with minimal government intervention argue that high marginal tax rates adversely affect individuals' incentives to work, save, and invest. High tax rates penalize success, discourage risk-taking, and impose a levy on some forms of income at literally confiscatory levels. A uniform rate avoids penalizing success. It ends bracket creep once and for all, and removes the penalty on marriage under the current system where different rates apply to single and married persons. The flat tax, set at a low rate, is the ultimate version of a supply-side tax system. The returns to all effort and savings are taxed at the same low rate. A flat rate provides the greatest encouragement to higher levels of work and investment.

The flat tax especially appeals to the American mainstream. Millions of Americans now troubled by the unfathomable complexity and high costs of compliance with the current tax system, who are offended by an upsurge in tax cheating, find the flat tax to be an attractive alternative. They especially like the idea that a tax return could fit on a postcard, taking a few minutes to complete and knowing that everyone was bound by the same rules. Two pages of instructions and a postcard-size form would replace a 44-page manual and 17 pages of schedules.

A flat tax strikes most Americans as a fair method of taxation. Tax all income once, and only once, at the same rate for all people. It seems manifestly unfair that some rich people pay no taxes, or that two families with the same income pay radically different amounts in taxes. Much of the middle class is stunned by the fact that they pay marginal tax rates approaching 50 percent, which only the upper classes paid 20 years ago. It would be hard to find anyone who would be willing to defend the current system as fair. In some respects, the perceived fairness of a flat tax conforms to the historical tithe, the 10 percent contribution all individuals were expected to donate to support church activities. Some of the flat-tax bills call for exactly a 10 percent rate with no deductions except for a small personal allowance.

Most Americans are disturbed about the rise in cheating. As more of their friends and neighbors hide or fail to report income, the temptation to join them increases. To resist is to be left holding the tax burden your neighbors have abandoned. The flat tax also seems to be the only promising vehicle to balance the federal budget, short of a constitutional amendment. The likelihood of federal budget deficits exceeding the hundred-billion dollar level for years to come, especially during a period of economic recovery, poses a severe threat to the nation's economic health. Almost nobody seriously believes it will ever be possible to balance the budget under the present tax system. Eliminating a few loopholes is not the answer, since members of Congress are likely to legislate new loopholes to benefit an endless list of new special interests just as quickly as they abolish old ones. Over time, the tax base has eroded significantly and our tax system, even at high rates, cannot raise enough revenue to balance the budget. A flat tax would end the erosion of the tax base. It could raise more revenue than the current system from low rates of tax, especially as the economy enjoys more rapid growth in the future. As we show in Chapter 5, a low flat rate of 19 percent would balance the budget by 1985. Even supply-siders, characterized by their earlier view that deficits don't matter, concede that a flat tax may be the only way out of the current budget crisis. The flat rate tax affords an opportunity to restore fiscal responsibility to the nation's public finances.

Apart from the desire to balance the budget, economists generally agree that the current high tax rate code distorts the flow of resources in the economy, with a net loss in economic welfare approaching $50 billion or more. More and more scholars take the view that the tax code should not be used as a tool of social policy, that it should concentrate on raising revenue. They argue that social policy should be implemented through the expenditure side of the budget. The preambles to several flat tax proposals offered by moderate Democrats accept the thesis that high tax rates damage investment and weaken the performance of our economy. It is not just the average or overall burden of taxation in the economy that bears on our well-being, but the structure of the tax system—as expressed in the form of high marginal rates—that may be more important still. Even such liberal Brookings Institution economists as Henry Aaron and Joseph Pechman agree that marginal rates of 50 percent are too high.

A true sign of the widespread appeal of the flat tax is the endorsement of the nation's leading papers—*The New York Times*, *Washington Post*, *Christian Science Monitor*, and other major dailies. They uniformly agree that the current system needs drastic overhaul and that further tinkering of the sort that took place in all nine postwar reforms would not help and might make matters worse.

Several existing grass-roots taxpayers' organizations—the National Taxpayers Union, the National Tax-Limitation Committee, the American Council on Capital Formation, the Council for a Competitive Economy, and the Chamber of Commerce—have said they support or will consider seriously working for the flat-rate tax. Milton Friedman likes the idea so much that he would prefer to see it sanctified in the form of a constitutional amendment.

No doubt, as yet unmentioned individuals and organizations like the flat tax for still other reasons. But the broadly-based coalition that has sprung up around the movement is beyond dispute. Supply-side officials in the Treasury who said little about it all throughout 1981 were quick to proclaim that they had always supported the flat-rate tax by mid-1982. Liberal economists who disdained a single-rate tax just three years ago now champion the virtue of postcard simplicity. Concern over uncontrollable budget deficits attracted orthodox budget-balancers to the flat tax as a means of raising additional revenue. And the American population at large has been attracted by the simplicity, fairness, and the inherent honesty such a system promises. Those with a vested interest in the current complex system will not find it easy to divide and conquer.

Progressivity and the Flat Tax

Opposition to a flat-rate tax has surfaced from several quarters. Intellectuals have charged that a flat tax of 20 percent or less would substantially shift the tax burden from wealthier to lower- and middle-income households. Congressional Budget Office Analyst Joseph Minarik has released statistics showing how tax payments would rise or fall for varying income classes under an 18.7 percent rate, assuming no changes in the economic behavior of these households as marginal rates fell. Some cartoonists have depicted the flat tax as a windfall for the rich. Even President Reagan's Treasury officials have said a flat tax would conflict with the long-standing principle that income taxes should be based on the person's ability to pay. Since 10 percent of taxpayers now pay 51.8 percent of all income taxes, opponents of the flat tax attribute this to the 50 percent marginal rates applied to their income. Our current progressive income tax system over the years has come to be equated with rising marginal or graduated tax rates levied on successively higher incomes.

Charges that a flat tax with no deductions would destroy our progressive income tax system are serious and deserve careful consideration. A first step is to develop a clear notion of the concept of progressivity as it applies to the working of federal income taxes. A tax system is progressive when it takes an increasing share of a taxpayer's income in taxes as that person's income rises. To illustrate, consider three families with incomes of $10,000, $20,000, and $30,000. Suppose the three families paid, respectively, taxes of $500, $2,000, and $4,500. The first family would thus pay 5 percent of its income in taxes, the second 10 percent, and the third 15 percent. Such payments would satisfy the definition of progressivity since families with larger incomes paid a higher share of their income in taxes than those with smaller incomes.

Now we can address the accusation that a flat tax would destroy our progressive income tax system. This criticism confuses the existence of a set of rising marginal rates as defining a progressive system with any rate structure in which the rich pay a higher percentage of their income in taxes. Graduated tax rates are not essential to progressivity.

First, all serious proponents of the flat-rate tax include some form of personal allowance for adults and their dependents. To eliminate loopholes does not mean ending the personal exemption. Once this point of the personal allowance is grasped, it is easy to see how a flat-rate tax generates an overall progressive income tax system.

Consider again the previous three families. Let's set the personal allowance for this hypothetical family of four—husband, wife, two children—at $10,000. The first family in our example would subtract its allowance of $10,000 from its income of $10,000, leaving no taxable income. Family one pays no taxes, or pays a zero percentage rate of its income in taxes.

Perform the same calculations for family two. Subtract its personal allowance of $10,000 from its $20,000 income, leaving taxable income of $10,000. At a 20 percent flat rate, family two would pay taxes of $2,000, which constitutes 10 percent of its total $20,000 income. Performing these computations for the $30,000 family generates $4,000 in taxes, which comes to 13.3 percent of family three's income. In the same straightforward fashion, families with successively higher incomes would pay a larger share of their income in taxes. At $40,000, the tax burden is 15 percent; at $50,000, 16 percent; and at $100,000, 18 percent. For very large incomes, the average tax rate begins to approach the flat marginal rate.

By now it should be clear that a flat-rate tax, in conjunction with a personal allowance, results in a progressive income tax system. The effective tax rate rises with each higher income group, thus satisfying the definition of progressivity. It is not necessary that tax rates be graduated to produce a progressive system.

Thus a flat-rate tax coupled with a personal allowance has the following desirable features:

- the poorest pay no income taxes at all;
- as income increases, a higher share of that income is paid in taxes, thus preserving the ability-to-pay principle; and
- all income is taxed at the same low marginal rate.

Raising or lowering the personal allowance increases or decreases the degree of progressivity in the system. Remember progressivity means that rich people pay a higher fraction of their income in taxes than poor people. It does not mean they must pay higher marginal tax rates on additional units of income. Do not equate graduated or steeply rising marginal tax rates with a progressive tax system.

Is the flat tax a windfall to the rich? The answer to this question depends on the details of different flat-tax plans. Our plan, set forth in Chapter 3, is not a windfall for the rich. We show in Chapter 4 that rich people currently escape taxation on a large portion of their income because of leakage in the present system. Corrected for leakage, rich people pay at much lower rates than reported in official IRS publications. Thus our plan would radically lower marginal rates, but not grant a windfall to the rich in overall tax savings. Moreover, we hope to persuade you that members of all income groups will be better off in a few years from the beneficial impact our flat-tax plan will have on the performance of the economy.

Historical Experience

The first income tax law of 1913 contained a graduated-rate surtax from one to 6 percent that was imposed on top of the "normal" one percent rate. Ever since, graduated rates have remained part and parcel of the personal income tax system. Top marginal rates have even reached the incredible 91 percent level at times in our history. Never have we employed a flat-rate tax, though the idea has surfaced from time to time as disenchantment has grown with our current system.

So we must look elsewhere to see how the flat tax has worked in practice. We have chosen three examples: the British experience in the nineteenth century, post-World War II Hong Kong, and the Isle of Guernsey, home of C. Northcote Parkinson.

Great Britain: 1842–1880

Throughout most of its history, Great Britain derived its revenue largely from customs and excise charges. To reform and reduce the tariff barriers to freer trade, Sir Robert Peel in 1842 introduced a "temporary" income tax (or, strictly speaking, reintroduced a tax that had been imposed as a temporary measure by William Pitt during the Napoleonic War between 1799 and 1815). As implemented, the tax imposed a charge of seven pence (7d.) in the pound. With 240 pence in the pound, this was a rate of 3 percent. Peel exempted all incomes below £150. Since per capita income in 1842 was £24, the income tax fell only on those with incomes sixfold the national average. For each pound over £150, the same 7d. rate applied. The tax yielded about £3.77 million of a total budget of £52 million.

Depending on the state of the nation's public finances, Chancellors of the Exchequer found occasion on which to raise or lower the standard rate, and raise or lower the level of exemption (or personal allowance). In some years, the standard rate reached a low of one percent (2d. in the pound). In other years the rate approached 7 percent (16d.). Typically, the rate averaged 2 to 3 percent. In general, the late nineteenth century was a period of steady economic growth and prosperity.

From 1880, two trends developed. First, graduated rates replaced the practice of a low standard rate. Second, the total tax burden rose sharply. Tax rates reached 30 percent during World War I, 50 percent during World War II, and exceeded 50 percent in the postwar years. Britain's economy has not performed well in the postwar era, leading some to conclude that high marginal tax rates have discouraged work, savings, and investment, and encouraged overseas migration of doctors, lawyers and professionals—a brain drain—and movement of capital abroad (despite stiff penalties).

Because of the large exemption in the nineteenth century, Britain's income tax then was a progressive system based on a standard flat rate. Low-income households paid no tax. Only those with incomes several-fold the national average paid any income taxes. As in our prior hypothetical examples, the average share of income paid in taxes rose with higher incomes.

For the historical record, it is interesting to note that William E. Gladstone, Chancellor of the Exchequer during the mid-1850s and early 1860s, then Prime Minister during portions of the 1870s and 1880s, tried to abolish the income tax. He had resolutely refused to graduate the income tax according to the size of income since this would constitute a penalty for hard work and enterprise. He never claimed that a tax rate of 4 percent would discourage productive economic activity. His chief concern was that the revenue such a tax could "painlessly" generate would encourage rising public expenditure and reduce efficiency in government. In just the ten years from 1875 to 1885, receipts from the income tax quadrupled, confirming his fears. He could not possibly have contemplated the high rates of, say, 50 percent that prevail in most Western countries today, a rate he would regard as confiscatory.

Hong Kong

Among industrial economies, Hong Kong is alone in using a flat-rate type income tax system. Hong Kong does not levy an overall income tax; instead it levies four separate direct taxes on profits, salaries, property, and interest. The maximum tax rate on corporate profits is 16.5 percent and 15 percent on unincorporated business profits, after deducting all expenses incurred in producing chargeable profits. The salaries tax is somewhat more complicated: the tax is imposed on a sliding-rate scale, ranging from a minimum of 5 percent on the first assessable HK$10,000 to 25 percent on taxable income exceeding HK$50,000. The income tax permits a very generous personal allowance. Also, the total tax due cannot exceed the standard rate of 15 percent of gross income. Thus at some point in the income ladder, the marginal rate drops from 25 to 15 percent. The standard rate zone, at which point taxpayers pay a flat 15 percent rate, varies with personal circumstances. For single persons, the standard rate of 15 percent takes hold at $20,000 (this amount and succeeding figures have been converted from Hong Kong dollars into U.S. dollars at August 1982 exchange rates of HK$6.00 = US$1.00); for married persons, $31,670; and for married persons with two children and two dependent parents, $43,800. The personal allowances for 1982 are:

Single:	$4,667
Married:	$9,334
Married with two children:	$11,584
Married with two children and two dependent parents:	$14,250

Personal allowances are far more generous in Hong Kong than in the United States. They are so generous that only 218,000 salaried taxpayers of a total population exceeding 5 million will bear any direct income tax liability in the 1982 tax year. Hong Kong illustrates the point that a standard 15 percent flat-rate tax accompanied by large personal allowances yields an extremely progressive system. Exactly 13,000 salaried taxpayers, about 6 percent of the total number in the salaried tax net, contribute over half the total yields from the salaries tax. Those who can afford to pay more do so. To repeat, the rich pay more on the basis of a standard rate of 15 percent on gross incomes in excess of $20,000 for single persons and in the range of $40,000 for married persons with dependents. The personal allowance is so large that the overwhelming majority of the population pay no income taxes whatsoever. Hong Kong clearly demonstrates how a flat rate and progressivity of the system go hand in hand.

Hong Kong also levies an interest tax of 10 percent at the source on Hong Kong dollar deposits—no tax is levied on foreign currency deposits. The payer of the interest deducts the tax and hands it directly to the Inland Revenue department. Finally, property tax, set at 15 percent of ratable value after an allowance for repairs and maintenance, is levied on the owner of investment property. Owner-occupants are exempt from the charge.

Apart from these four direct taxes, the Hong Kong government collects revenue from land and property sales, stamp and excise duties, and fees and charges for publicly supplied commercial services. The relative composition of total revenue varies from year to year. However, the experience of Hong Kong from a low standard rate of 16.5 percent on corporate profits and 15 percent on salaries, interest, and unincorporated business profits would surprise almost everyone. Virtually without exception, Hong Kong runs a huge budget surplus every year. By running budget surpluses in 31 of the last 34 years, the government has accumulated a huge reserve of funds, rather than a colossal national debt. These accumulated reserves are equal to about half of all government spending for the 1982–83 budget year. In the

United States, high marginal tax rates have accompanied annual budget deficits now surpassing $100 billion. We have had deficits in 41 of the last 50 years, and in 19 of the last 20 years. Compare the Hong Kong situation with the total national debt in the United States, which equals about one and a half years' worth of current federal spending.

Financial authorities in Hong Kong have consistently stressed one tenet of tax policy: low standard rates of direct taxation facilitate rapid economic growth. Revenue yields from rapid growth are sufficient to finance an extremely ambitious program of public expenditure on housing, education, health, welfare, and other social and community services. A succession of financial secretaries, the counterpart to our secretary of the treasury, chairman of the Council of Economic Advisers, and chairman of the Federal Reserve Board rolled into one, have repeated the message: investment is stimulated by low rates of direct taxation.

Their words merit reproduction. Arthur Clarke, financial secretary during the 1950s, cautioned in his outgoing year: "We would do well to delay an increase in our direct taxation rate, the low level of which is such an incentive to our expanding economy, on which in turn we depend for increasing revenue." His successor, Sir John Cowperthwaite, in 1964, asserted the same principle: "That revenue has increased in this way is in no small measure, I am convinced, due to our low tax policy which has helped to generate an economic expansion in the face of unfavorable circumstances. . . . Economic expansion remains the door to social progress and I am convinced that low taxation can in general produce a greater growth in revenue than can tax increases."

To summarize, low taxes stimulate investment and rapid economic growth. Low tax rates are consonant with budget surpluses, not deficits. They permit steady growth in public spending, not sharp contractions. In the past 20 years, real economic growth in Hong Kong has averaged 9 percent; since 1976, it has grown at the even more incredible rate of 10.7 percent, the industrial world's highest rate. Speak to any businessman, investor, banker, government official, or scholar in Hong Kong and he will tell you that low rates of taxation are a key to its economic growth and steadily rising prosperity.

The Isle of Guernsey

In January 1981, John Train, a consulting editor to *Forbes* Magazine, interviewed C. Northcote Parkinson on the general subject of Parkinsons's rules. One rule involved the destructive effects of heavy taxation on both government revenue and individual work effort.

The cause of bad government, he noted, lay in the process of adding up from the bottom all government spending to yield a total budget. Such a budget is, of course, overstated and invariably more than a country can afford. The correct procedure is to calculate the largest amount of revenue the government can reasonably collect— meaning a low *rate* of taxation—and then allocate that amount among the different departments. Noting that most countries were not well governed as evidenced by high rates of inflation, Parkinson was asked to give an example of good government.

He offered the example of his home island of Guernsey, which adhered to his correct principles of public finance. First, the government never spent money it didn't have. Second, the tax rate was set at a low, flat 20 percent (after allowing for business deductions). Formerly, he noted, the rate was 25 percent, "which was reduced in order to increase revenues. I have no doubt at all that if it was reduced to 15 percent it would further increase revenues." As a result, the average Guernseyman works about 56 hours a week. Anyone working that long would be a good deal more prosperous than one who works only 40 hours a week and clamors for even less.

In the chapters that follow, we describe our flat-rate tax plan. By granting personal allowances, it is a progressive system. It also provides incentives for savings, thus laying the foundation for faster economic growth in the future. We then review the impact of our plan on the housing industry, charitable contributions, to what extent any shift in the tax burden occurs, and how the transition to our plan would occur. We try to anticipate and answer dozens of concrete questions about how the simple, flat tax would differ in practice from the current system. Finally we compare our plan with other flat-rate proposals that have been introduced as bills in Congress.

3 CHAPTER

A Practical, Low, Simple, Flat Tax

Here is a concise statement of what we are looking for in a sensible tax system:

1. All income should be taxed only once, as close as possible to its source.
2. All types of income should be taxed at the same low rate.
3. The poorest families should pay no tax, and lower-income families should pay a smaller fraction of their incomes in tax than do those with higher incomes.
4. Tax returns for both families and businesses should be simple enough to fit on postcards.

The first principle seems obvious enough, but the tax system of the U.S. today violates it repeatedly. Some kinds of income—like fringe benefits—are never taxed at all. Other kinds, like dividends, are taxed twice. And interest income, which is supposed to be taxed once, actually escapes taxation completely in all too many cases, where clever taxpayers arrange to receive interest in a way that escapes the income tax. You can make an interest-free loan to your daughter, for example, and let her invest the money in a bond whose interest will be taxed at her income tax rate, which may be zero. And then she can spend the interest on some things that you would have paid for anyway, like piano lessons.

Taxing all income at the same rate, the second principle, is the crux of the flat-rate tax. Its logic is much more profound than just the simplicity of the tax calculation with a single tax rate. Whenever different forms of income face different tax rates, or different taxpayers face different tax rates, the public takes full advantage of the opportunities to receive income in ways involving low rates. When the tax system permits deductions, you can be sure that the deductions will be taken against the income that pays the highest tax. Here are some examples of transactions attributable to differences in tax rates:

- Employers offer workers stock options instead of cash salaries, because the option will eventually be taxed at lower capital gain rates.

- A real estate operator borrows from a savings and loan association. He deducts the interest at his 50 percent marginal rate, but the interest received by the depositors at the savings and loan is taxed at their lower rate.
- An author arranges for royalties to be deferred because she knows she will be in a lower tax bracket next year.
- A profitable corporation is liquidated in order to avoid the high corporate income tax on its earnings.
- A wealthy man arranges for all the support to his former wife and children to be paid as alimony, so it is deductible at his high tax rate and taxable at his former wife's lower rate.

All these inequities and inefficiencies can be swept away in one stroke by imposing equal tax rates on all income.

Limiting the burden of taxes on the poor is a central principle of tax reform. Tax systems like a federal sales tax or a value-added tax on businesses make all citizens, rich and poor alike, pay essentially the same fraction of their incomes in taxes. The current federal tax system avoids taxing the poor, and we think it should stay that way. But again we stress that exempting the poor does not require graduated tax rates, rising to high levels for upper-income families. Graduated taxes automatically create differences among taxpayers in tax rates, and the attendant opportunities for leakage. A flat rate, applied to all income above a generous personal allowance, provides progressivity without creating differences in tax rates.

Simplicity of tax forms and tax laws is not just a matter of limiting the deforestation of America through the Internal Revenue Service's appetite for paper. Complicated taxes require expensive advisors for taxpayers and equally expensive review and audit by the government. A complicated tax invites the taxpayer to search for a special feature that can be twisted to escape the taxation of some income or give an advantageous deduction to some expense. And complicated taxes diminish confidence in government, inviting a breakdown in cooperation with the tax system and widespread outright evasion.

The Proposed Reform

This chapter builds the case that we have developed a completely new tax system faithful to all four of our principles. Though our system has two separate taxes—one on business income and the other on wages and salaries—it is important to think of it as an integrated system. When we speak of its virtues, like its equal taxation of all types of income, we mean the system, not one of its two parts.

In our system, all income in the country is classified as either business income or wages and salaries. The system is watertight; the taxes on both types of income are equal. Progressivity is a feature of just the wage and salary tax. The forms for both taxes will fit on postcards. The low tax rate of 19 percent is enough to match the revenue of the federal tax system as it existed in 1980, and enough to balance the federal budget by 1985 under current spending plans.

Though our business and wage-salary taxes will replace the present corporate and personal income taxes, do not think of our business tax as the replacement for the corporate tax and our wage-salary tax as the replacement for the personal income tax. Many types of businesses besides corporations will file our business tax form. Even within corporations, vastly more income is covered by our business tax than today's corporate income tax. In 1981, the revenue from the corporate income tax with a tax rate of 46 percent was $57 billion. The revenue from our business tax at a rate of only 19 percent would have been $157 billion, almost three times as high even though the tax rate is well under half the corporate rate.

The other side of the coin, of course, is that our wage-salary tax yields less revenue than the current personal income tax—$194 billion in 1981 against $289 billion. But don't think we are proposing a massive shift in taxes from wages to capital income. Our wage-salary tax applies just to wages, salaries, and private pensions, whereas today's personal income tax includes unincorporated business income, dividends, interest, rent, and many other kinds of income we put under our business tax instead.

The question we are always asked when we try to explain our system is: Why don't families have to pay tax on their interest, dividends, and other unearned income? Isn't this a tremendous break for the wealthy, who get the vast bulk of that kind of income? The point is that our system does tax this kind of income, at the same rate as all income. Though we will start by describing the compensation tax on individuals and families, the way that our complete system taxes all income uniformly won't become clear until we cover the business tax, the most novel part of our proposal.

The Individual Compensation Tax

The individual compensation tax has a single purpose—to tax the large fraction of total income paid as cash by employers to workers. It is not a tax system in itself, but one of two major parts of a complete system.

For the tax, compensation is defined precisely and narrowly as actual payments of wages, salaries, and pensions. Pension contributions and other fringe benefits paid by employers are not counted as part of compensation. In other words, the tax is paid when the retired worker actually receives the pension, not when the employer sets aside the money to pay the future pension.

The tax return for the compensation tax is almost self-explanatory:

HALL-RABUSHKA SIMPLIFIED FLAT-RATE TAX FORM

Form 1	Individual Compensation Tax	1982
Your first name and initial (if joint return, also give spouse's name and initial)	Last name	Your social security number
Present home address (Number and street, including apartment number, or rural route)		Spouse's social security no
City, town or post office, State and ZIP code	Your occupation ►	
	Spouse's occupation ►	

1	Compensation as reported by employer	1	
2	Other wage income, including pensions	2	
3	Total compensation *(line 1 plus line 2)*	3	
4	Personal allowance		
	(a) ☐ $6200 for married filing jointly	4(a)	
	(b) ☐ $3800 for single	4(b)	
	(c) ☐ $5600 for single head of household	4(c)	
5	Number of dependents, not including spouse	5	
6	Personal allowances for dependents *(line 5 multiplied by $750)*	6	
7	Total personal allowances *(line 4 plus line 6)*	7	
8	Taxable compensation *(line 3 less line 7)*	8	
9	Tax *(19% of line 8)*	9	
10	Tax withheld by employer	10	
11	Tax due *(line 9 less line 10, if positive)*	11	
12	Refund due *(line 10 less line 9, if positive)*	12	

To limit the burden of the tax on poor families, only earnings above a personal allowance are taxed. The allowance is $7700 for a family of four in 1982, but would grow along with the cost of living in later years. All the taxpayer has to do is report total wages, salaries, and pensions at the top, compute the personal allowance based on marital status and number of dependents, subtract the allowance, multiply by

19 percent to compute the tax, take account of withholding, and pay the difference or apply for a refund. For about 80 percent of the population, filling out this postcard once a year would be the only effort imposed on them by the federal tax system. What a change from the many pages of schedules filled out by the typical frustrated taxpayer today!

At a low flat rate of 19 percent, the individual compensation tax generates a large fraction of the revenue needed by the federal government. In 1981, wages, salaries, and private pensions were about $1603 billion. Personal allowances that would have been deducted were about $481 billion (this estimate takes into account the number of people who would not be able to deduct the full amount of the allowance because their earnings were below the allowance). Tax revenues would have been $194 billion. For comparison, the personal income tax produced $289 billion in revenue in 1981.

For the 80 percent or so of the population who receive no business income directly, the individual compensation tax is the only tax they will have to worry about. Many features of current taxes will disappear. Charitable deductions will no longer exist—we will have much more to say on this controversial subject in the next chapter. Deductions for mortgage and other interest payments will vanish, as part of the general plan to put all interest payments on an after-tax basis, an aspect of the business tax we will explain shortly. On the other hand, deductions for business expenses for people like commission salesmen are permitted, because they are among the 20 percent who file the business tax return.

Again we stress that the compensation tax is not a complete income tax on individuals. It taxes only wages, salaries, and pensions. The companion business tax picks up all other components of income. Together they form a watertight tax system.

The Business Tax

In the first place, the purpose of the business tax is not to tax businesses. Fundamentally, people pay taxes, not businesses. The idea of the business tax is to collect the tax that the owners of a business owe on the income produced by the business. Collecting business income at its source avoids the single biggest source of leakage in the tax system today, the avoidance and outright evasion of income tax on interest and dividends. Watertight taxation of individual business income at the source in the business is possible because we already know the tax rate of all of the owners of the business—it is the common flat rate paid by all taxpayers. If the tax system had graduated rates, taxation at the source would be difficult or impossible. Suppose there were three or four different rates, as some modified flat-rate proposals call for. Then the business would have to find out the tax rate applicable to each of its owners, and apply that rate to the income produced in the business for that owner. The form would have at least five more lines for these computations. But that is only the beginning of the problem. The Internal Revenue Service would have to audit a business and its owners together in order to see that the owners were reporting the correct tax rates to the business. Further, suppose one of the owners made a mistake, and later discovered he was in a higher tax bracket. Then the business would have to refile its tax form to collect the right tax. Obviously this wouldn't work. Business taxes have to be collected from the owners, not from the source, if tax rates are graduated. This is a powerful practical reason for a flat-rate tax.

The business tax is a giant, comprehensive withholding tax on all types of income other than wages, salaries, and pensions. It is carefully designed to tax every bit of income outside of compensation, but to tax it only once. The business tax does not have deductions for interest payments, dividends, or any other type of payment to the owners of the business. As a result, all income that people receive from business activity has already been taxed. Because it has already extracted its tax, the tax system need not worry about what happens to interest or dividends after they leave the firm. The resulting simplification and improvement in the tax system is enormous. To take just a single example, the Internal Revenue Service currently puts a great deal of effort into keeping track of trusts. A trust receives interest and dividend income, and the beneficiary of the trust is supposed to pay income tax on that income. Naturally, it is tricky to check that this is being done, and, in any case, if the beneficiary is a child in a low tax bracket, the trust is just a gimmick to take advantage of differences in tax rates. With our business tax, people can be as creative as they want in setting up trusts; the tax is paid before the money arrives at the trust and the Internal Revenue Service can relax. This is really important to the typical person who does not take advantage of trusts, because it increases the taxes paid by those inclined toward gimmicks and avoidance, and so lowers the taxes paid by the typical person.

The way that we have chosen to set up the business tax is not at all arbitrary—on the contrary, it is virtually dictated by the principles we set forth at the beginning of this chapter. The tax is to bear on all the income originating in the business, but is not to tax any income that originates in other businesses, nor is it to tax the wages, salaries, and pensions it pays to its employees. The types of income taxed by the business tax include:

- profits from the use of plant and equipment;
- profits from ideas embodied in copyrights, patents, trade secrets, and the like;
- profits from past marketing and advertising efforts;
- earnings of key executives and others who are owners as well as employees, and who are paid less than they contribute to the business;
- earnings of doctors, lawyers, and other professionals;
- rent earned from apartments and offices;
- fringe benefits provided to workers.

The business tax works in the following way: All income derives fundamentally from the sale of the products and services produced by the business. On the top line of the business tax form goes the gross sales of the business—the proceeds it received from the sale of all of its products. But some of the proceeds amount to the resale of things the firm purchased; the tax is already paid on them because the seller also has to pay the business tax. So the firm can deduct the cost of all the goods, materials, and services it purchases for the purpose of making the product it sells. In addition, it can deduct its wages, salaries, and pensions, for the taxes on these will be paid by the people receiving them, under our compensation tax. Finally, the business can deduct all its outlays for plant, equipment, and land. A little later we will explain why this investment incentive is just the right one.

Everything left from this calculation is the income originating in the firm, and is taxed at the flat rate of 19 percent. In most American businesses, a lot is left, and the revenue from the business tax is substantial. Many deductions allowed business under current laws are eliminated in our plan—these include interest payments, state and local taxes, and fringe benefits. But our exclusion of these deductions is not an arbitrary move to increase the tax base. In all cases, the elimination of deductions, when combined with the other features of our system, moves toward the goal of taxing all income once at a common, low rate.

Eliminating the deduction of interest paid by businesses is a central part of our general plan to tax income at the source. It makes sense because we do not propose to tax the interest receipts of individuals. The tax that the government hopes that individuals will pay (often vainly) is paid for sure by the business itself.

We sweep away the whole complicated apparatus of depreciation deductions, but we replace it with something more favorable for capital formation, immediate 100 percent first-year tax writeoff of all investment spending. We don't deny depreciation deductions; we enhance them. More on this shortly.

The elimination of deductions for state and local taxes holds both for the business tax and for the individual compensation tax. The present system with full deductions encourages people to get some of their economic services through state and local governments, rather than in the private marketplace. A town is better off financing its trash collection through deductible taxes on businesses and families than through nondeductible payments from families to private trash collection services. Elimination of deductions makes the town neutral in the choice, as it should be.

Fringe benefits are outside the current tax system completely, which makes no sense. The cost of fringes is deductible by businesses, but workers are not taxed on the value of fringes. Consequently fringes have a big advantage over cash wages. As taxation has become heavier and heavier, fringes have become more and more important in the total package offered by employers to workers—fringes were only 1.2 percent of total compensation in 1929, when income taxes were unimportant, as against 16.3 percent in 1981. The explosion of fringes is strictly an artifact of taxation, and is an economically inefficient way to pay people. Were the tax system neutral, taxing fringes at the same rate as cash wages, people would rather take their income in cash and make their own decisions about health and life insurance, country club dues, exercise facilities, and all the other things they get now from their employers without much choice. Furthermore, failing to tax fringes means taxes on other types of income are all the higher. Bringing all types of income under the tax system is essential for low rates.

Here is the simple form each business would file under our system:

HALL-RABUSHKA SIMPLIFIED FLAT RATE TAX FORM

Form 2	Business Tax	1982
Business Name		Employer Identification Number
Street Address		County
City, State, and ZIP Code		Principal Product

1 Gross revenue from sales	1	
2 Allowable costs		
(a) Purchases of goods, services, and materials	2(a)	. . . .
(b) Wages, salaries, and pensions paid to employees.	2(b)	. . . .
(c) Purchases of capital equipment, structures, and land	2(c)	. . . .
3 Total allowable costs *(sum of lines 2(a), 2(b), 2(c)*	3	
4 Taxable income *(line 1 less line 3)*	4	
5 Tax *(19% of line 4)*	5	
6 Carry-forward from 1981	6	
7 Interest on carry-forward *(14% of line 6)*	7	. . . .
8 Carry-forward into 1982 *(line 6 plus line 7)*	8	
9 Tax due *(line 5 less line 8, if positive)*	9	
10 Carry-forward to 1983 *(line 8 less line 5, if positive)*	10	

Even the largest business—the Exxon Corporation in 1981 with $113 billion in sales—would fill out this simple postcard form. Every line on the form is a straightforward, well-defined number obtained directly from the business's accounting records. Line 1, gross revenue from sales, is the actual number of dollars received from the sales of all the products and services of the business, plus the proceeds from the sale of plant, equipment, and land. Line 2a is the actual amount paid for all the inputs necessary for the operation of the business. The firm could report essentially anything it purchased provided it was actually needed for its products and was not being given to the employees or owners. Line 2b is the actual cash put in the hands of workers and former workers. Everything deducted on this line must be reported by the workers in their compensation tax returns. Line 2c reports purchases of new and used capital equipment, buildings, and land. Note that the firm doesn't have to agonize over whether a screwdriver is a capital investment or a current input—both are deductible, and the government doesn't care which line it appears on.

    The taxable income computed on line 4 bears little resemblance to anybody's notion of profit. The business tax is not a profit tax. When Apple Computer is having an outstanding year in sales and profits, but is building new factories to handle rapid growth, it may well have a low or even negative taxable income. That's fine—later, when expansion slows but sales are at a high level, the income generated at Apple will be taxed at 19 percent and will make its appropriate contribution to financing the federal government.

Because the business tax treats investment in plant, equipment, and land as an expense, companies in the startup period will have negative taxable income. But the government does not write a check for the negative tax on the negative income—whenever the government starts writing checks, clever people will abuse the opportunity through fraud and legal maneuvers. Instead, the negative tax is carried forward to future years, when the business should have positive taxable income. There is no limit to the number of years of carry-forward. Moreover, balances carried forward earn the market rate of interest (14 percent in 1981, but probably less in more normal years). Lines 6 through 10 show the mechanics of the carry-forward process.

Examples

The easiest way to explain the practical operation of the business tax is through some examples. To start at the top, here is the business tax return for the mighty Exxon Corporation:

HALL-RABUSHKA SIMPLIFIED FLAT RATE TAX FORM

Form 2	Business Tax	1982

Business Name	Employer Identification Number
Exxon Corporation	48-29956

Street Address	County
1251 Avenue of the Americas	New York

City, State, and ZIP Code	Principal Product
New York, New York 10020	Oil

1 Gross revenue from sales	1	113,196,747,000
2 Allowable costs		
(a) Purchases of goods, services, and materials	2(a)	64,323,796,000
(b) Wages, salaries, and pensions paid to employees	2(b)	18,582,720,000
(c) Purchases of capital equipment, structures, and land	2(c)	5,783,472,000
3 Total allowable costs (sum of lines 2(a), 2(b), 2(c))	3	88,689,390,000
4 Taxable income (line 1 less line 3)	4	24,507,350,000
5 Tax (19% of line 4)	5	4,656,396,000
6 Carry-forward from 1981	6	0
7 Interest on carry-forward (14% of line 6)	7	0
8 Carry-forward into 1982 (line 6 plus line 7)	8	0
9 Tax due (line 5 less line 8, if positive)	9	4,656,396,000
10 Carry-forward to 1983 (line 8 less line 5, if positive)	10	0

We filled out this return from Exxon's annual report, which includes the activities of its overseas subsidiaries. Overseas subsidiaries are outside the scope of the new business tax and will be discussed later in the chapter. Had Exxon been entirely domestic, it would have paid about $4.7 billion in business tax. In fact, it paid just over $4 billion in income taxes to the U.S. and other governments in 1981. Even though the simple tax has a much lower rate—19 percent against 46 percent for the U.S. corporate income tax and similar rates in other countries—it actually raises more revenue because of its much more inclusive base.

Second is Apple Computer:

HALL-RABUSHKA SIMPLIFIED FLAT RATE TAX FORM

Form 2	Business Tax		1982

Business Name Apple Computer, Inc.		Employer Identification Number 78-84664	
Street Address 10495 Bandley Drive		County Santa Clara	
City, State, and ZIP Code Cupertino, California		Principal Product Microcomputers	

1 Gross revenue from sales		1	334,783,000
2 Allowable costs			
(a) Purchases of goods, services, and materials		2(a)	180,361,000
(b) Wages, salaries, and pensions paid to employees		2(b)	88,279,000
(c) Purchases of capital equipment, structures, and land		2(c)	24,529,000
3 Total allowable costs (sum of lines 2(a), 2(b), 2(c))		3	293,169,000
4 Taxable income (line 1 less line 3)		4	41,614,000
5 Tax (19% of line 4)		5	7,906,660
6 Carry-forward from 1981		6	0
7 Interest on carry-forward (14% of line 6)		7	0
8 Carry-forward into 1982 (line 6 plus line 7)		8	0
9 Tax due (line 5 less line 8, if positive)		9	7,906,660
10 Carry-forward to 1983 (line 8 less line 5, if positive)		10	0

Actual income tax: $37,123,000
Source Apple Computer, Inc., 1981 Annual Report

Because Apple is investing and growing rapidly, its taxes are low— it benefits tremendously from the first-year writeoff for investment. Its tax of $7.9 million is a small fraction of the actual income tax Apple paid in 1981 of $37.1 million.

Now for some smaller businesses and activities that are taxed under the business tax, even though they may not usually be called businesses. Sanford and Sigrid Seigneur are a prosperous couple who bought an apartment building a few years ago. Here is what their business return for the building would look like under the assumption that the business tax had been in effect from the year they bought the building:

HALL-RABUSHKA SIMPLIFIED FLAT RATE TAX FORM

Form 2	Business Tax	1982

Business Name	Employer Identification Number
SANFORD and SIGRID SEIGNEUR	14-08041

Street Address	County
435 RIVERSIDE DRIVE	ATCHISON

City, State, and ZIP Code	Principal Product
ATCHISON, KANSAS	APARTMENT RENTALS

1 Gross revenue from sales	1	47,312
2 Allowable costs		
(a) Purchases of goods, services, and materials	2(a)	3,986
(b) Wages, salaries, and pensions paid to employees	2(b)	0
(c) Purchases of capital equipment, structures, and land	2(c)	0
3 Total allowable costs *(sum of lines 2(a), 2(b), 2(c))*	3	3,986
4 Taxable income *(line 1 less line 3)*	4	43,326
5 Tax *(19% of line 4)*	5	8,232
6 Carry-forward from 1981	6	53,907
7 Interest on carry-forward *(14% of line 6)*	7	7,547
8 Carry-forward into 1982 *(line 6 plus line 7)*	8	61,454
9 Tax due *(line 5 less line 8, if positive)*	9	0
10 Carry-forward to 1983 *(line 8 less line 5, if positive)*	10	53,222

The gross revenue they report is just the total of the rent paid by their various tenants. Their costs are just the total of payments to the plumber for the frozen pipe in February 1982, their insurance premiums, and a handful of other expenses. Neither the interest on the mortgage they have on the property nor their property tax bills are counted as costs. Their tax for this year, $8232, is substantial, but they still have a large carry-forward from the purchase of the building, so they don't actually pay anything this year. As time goes by, the carry-forward will probably decline (depending on what happens to rents and interest rates), and they will begin to pay tax. If they sell the building, they will have to include the proceeds of the sale on line 1, and pay 19 percent of the sale price less any remaining carry-forward at that time.

Seymour Krankheit is a successful pediatric neurosurgeon:

HALL-RABUSHKA SIMPLIFIED FLAT RATE TAX FORM

Form 2	Business Tax	1982

Business Name	Seymour Krankheit , MD	Employer Identification Number	97-01469
Street Address	1948 Prospect Road	County	Dallas
City, State, and ZIP Code	Dallas Texas	Principal Product	Medical Services

1 Gross revenue from sales		1	228,163
2 Allowable costs			
(a) Purchases of goods, services, and materials		2(a)	78,451
(b) Wages, salaries, and pensions paid to employees		2(b)	47,328
(c) Purchases of capital equipment, structures, and land		2(c)	10,409
3 Total allowable costs (sum of lines 2(a), 2(b), 2(c))		3	136,194
4 Taxable income (line 1 less line 3)		4	91,969
5 Tax (19% of line 4)		5	17,474
6 Carry-forward from 1981		6	0
7 Interest on carry-forward (14% of line 6)		7	0
8 Carry-forward into 1982 (line 6 plus line 7)		8	0
9 Tax due (line 5 less line 8, if positive)		9	17,474
10 Carry-forward to 1983 (line 8 less line 5, if positive)		10	0

His gross revenue is the amount he collects from insurance companies, Medicare and Medicaid, and the occasional unlucky patient who still pays his own medical bills. He also receives a salary as a hospital employee, but that income is not reported here; it belongs on his individual compensation tax return, Form 1. All the costs of running his office are included in allowable costs except the fringe benefits he provides his nurse and himself. In the old days when he was a professional corporation, he could deduct tens of thousands of dollars as contributions to his own pension plan, but the Hall-Rabushka reform has eliminated that abuse. He could still be a professional corporation if he wanted, but it wouldn't have any tax advantages. Even though he used to be in the 50 percent bracket under the old personal income tax, and now he pays only the 19 percent rate, he is now paying more tax.

Sally Vendeuse works as a manufacturers' representative—she is a traveling saleswoman:

HALL-RABUSHKA SIMPLIFIED FLAT RATE TAX FORM

Form 2	Business Tax	1982

Business Name	Employer Identification Number
Sally Vendeuse	*15-13255*

Street Address	County
903 S Ashland	*Lancaster*

City, State, and ZIP Code	Principal Product
Lancaster, PA	*Sales Services*

1 Gross revenue from sales	1	*68,147*
2 Allowable costs		
(a) Purchases of goods, services, and materials	2(a)	*10,317*
(b) Wages, salaries, and pensions paid to employees	2(b)	*0*
(c) Purchases of capital equipment, structures, and land	2(c)	*10,942*
3 Total allowable costs *(sum of lines 2(a), 2(b), 2(c)*	3	*21,259*
4 Taxable income *(line 1 less line 3)*	4	*46,888*
5 Tax *(19% of line 4)*	5	*8,909*
6 Carry-forward from 1981	6	*0*
7 Interest on carry-forward *(14% of line 6)*	7	*0*
8 Carry-forward into 1982 *(line 6 plus line 7)*	8	*0*
9 Tax due *(line 5 less line 8, if positive)*	9	*8,909*
10 Carry-forward to 1983 *(line 8 less line 5, if positive)*	10	*0*

Her gross revenue on line 1 is the commissions she earns. Her allowable costs include all of her travel expenses, and the costs of taking her customers to lunch. She keeps careful records to show that her trips are for business and not for skiing, and that the lunches are to sweet-talk her customers, not her friends. On line 3c, she has deducted the full cost of a Honda Accord she bought for business use. She could have paid herself a salary of any amount she chose, and if she were single, she would have paid herself at least $3800 to take advantage of the personal allowance in the compensation tax, but her husband earns a salary as a nursery school teacher, so there is no need for a salary for her.

Samuel Agricola had the bad luck to be a farmer in Iowa in 1982:

HALL-RABUSHKA SIMPLIFIED FLAT RATE TAX FORM

Form 2	Business Tax	1982

Business Name **Samuel Agricola**	Employer Identification Number **53-89617**
Street Address **Rural Route 2**	County **Keokuk**
City, State, and ZIP Code **Gibson City, IOWA**	Principal Product **CORN**

1 Gross revenue from sales....................................	1	*111 635*
2 Allowable costs		
(a) Purchases of goods, services, and materials	2(a)	*78,203*
(b) Wages, salaries, and pensions paid to employees............	2(b)	*33,844*
(c) Purchases of capital equipment, structures, and land	2(c)	*7,612*
3 Total allowable costs *(sum of lines 2(a), 2(b), 2(c))*	3	*119,659*
4 Taxable income *(line 1 less line 3)*	4	*−8024*
5 Tax *(19% of line 4)*.......................................	5	*−1525*
6 Carry-forward from 1981	6	*0*
7 Interest on carry-forward *(14% of line 6)*	7	*0*
8 Carry-forward into 1982 *(line 6 plus line 7)*....................	8	*0*
9 Tax due *(line 5 less line 8, if positive)*	9	*0*
10 Carry-forward to 1983 *(line 8 less line 5, if positive)*	10	*1525*

corn and other crops he grows. It fell a little short of what he paid to his suppliers and workers. The government will let him take the $1525 carry-forward against future taxes, when the normal profitability of his farm is restored.

The Galloping Grocer is a corner grocery run by a married couple with a few part-time employees (*see facing page*):

Its costs include the wholesale costs of the products on its shelves, its utility bills and rent, but, again, not its interest costs or its taxes. For the shaving cream and other items on which it collects state sales tax, it includes the tax in its gross revenue but does not report the tax as a cost—the federal government collects a tax of 19 percent on the sales tax. On line 2b, the couple includes salaries for themselves totaling $8450 so that they can take advantage of the personal allowances for themselves and their three children under the compensation tax.

Investment Incentives

The high tax rates of the current tax system significantly impede capital formation. On this point almost everybody agrees. The government's solution to the problem has been to pile one special incentive on another, creating a complex and unworkable maze of regulations and tax forms. Existing investment incentives are appallingly uneven in their effect. Capital projects taking full advantage of accelerated depreciation, the investment tax credit, and the deductibility of interest are actually *subsidized* by the government, not taxed at all. But equity-financed projects not eligible for fast depreciation are taxed heavily. Investment incentives severely distort the flow of capital into the most favored areas.

We propose to start over by throwing away all of the present incentives and replacing them with a simple, uniform principle—the total amount of investment is treated as an expense in the year it is made. The first virtue of this reform is simplicity. The business and the government need not quarrel, as they do now, over what is an investment and what is a current expense. The distinction doesn't matter for the tax. Complicated depreciation calculations, carrying over from one year to the next and driving the small business owner to distraction and the expense of professional tax assistance, vanish from the tax form. The even more complicated provisions for recapturing depreciation when a piece of equipment or a building is sold will vanish as well, to everyone's relief. All the complexities of the investment

HALL-RABUSHKA SIMPLIFIED FLAT RATE TAX FORM

Form 2	Business Tax	1982

Business Name *The Galloping Grocer*	Employer Identification Number *69-96060*
Street Address *Old Highway Road*	County *Santa Cruz*
City, State, and ZIP Code *Watsonville, Ca*	Principal Product *Retail groceries*

1 Gross revenue from sales	1		*515,921*
2 Allowable costs			
(a) Purchases of goods, services, and materials	2(a)		*469,133*
(b) Wages, salaries, and pensions paid to employees	2(b)		*29,411*
(c) Purchases of capital equipment, structures, and land	2(c)		*1,496*
3 Total allowable costs *(sum of lines 2(a), 2(b), 2(c)*	3		*500,040*
4 Taxable income *(line 1 less line 3)*	4		*15,881*
5 Tax *(19% of line 4)*	5		*3017*
6 Carry-forward from 1981	6		*0*
7 Interest on carry-forward *(14% of line 6)*	7		*0*
8 Carry-forward into 1982 *(line 6 plus line 7)*	8		*0*
9 Tax due *(line 5 less line 8, if positive)*	9		*3017*
10 Carry-forward to 1983 *(line 8 less line 5, if positive)*	10		*0*

credit—what investments are eligible, whether the project lasts long enough to earn the full credit, what fraction of a plant is actually equipment and therefore receives the credit, and the recapture of the credit when an asset is sold—disappear along with the credit.

Expensing of investment has a much deeper rationale than simplicity. Every act of investment in the economy ultimately traces back to an act of saving. Exempting investment from taxation is the same thing as exempting saving. A tax on income with an exemption for saving is in effect a tax on consumption, for consumption is the difference between income and saving. Consumption is what people take out of the economy; income is what people contribute to the economy. A consumption tax is the exact embodiment of the principle that people should be taxed on what they take out, not what they put in. The simple tax, with expensing of investment, is precisely a consumption tax.

Expensing investment eliminates the double taxation of saving; this is another way to express the most economically significant feature of expensing. Under an income tax, people pay tax once when they earn and save, and pay tax again as the savings earn a return. With expensing, the first tax is abolished. Saving is in effect deducted in computing the tax. Later, the return to the saving is taxed, through the business tax. Though economists have dreamt up a number of other ways to eliminate double taxation of saving (most involving complicated record-keeping and reporting by individuals), the technique exploited in the simple tax is by far the most straightforward.

Capital Gains

Capital gains on rental property, plant, and equipment are taxed under the business tax. The purchase price is deducted at the time of purchase, and the sale price is taxed at the time of the sale. Every owner of rental real estate would be required to fill out the simple business tax return.

Capital gains in the overall value of a successful firm are also taxed under the new business tax and should not be taxed again at the household level. To see this point, consider the case of the common stock of a corporation. The value of its stock in the market is the capitalization of its future earnings. Because the owners of the stock receive the earnings after the corporation has paid the business tax, that tax depresses the stock's market value. When the market learns that future earnings are likely to be higher than previously thought, the stock rises in value and its owners receive capital gains. When the high earnings materialize in the future, they will be correspondingly taxed. To tax the immediate capital gains of the stock would be double taxation. Thus with comprehensive taxation of business income at the source, capital gains should be excluded from taxation at the household level.

Capital gains on owner-occupied houses are not taxed under the simple flat tax. In the simple tax system, all taxation of owner-occupied housing is ceded to state and local governments, and none is attempted by the federal government. Most local governments tax houses quite heavily. The market value of a house is the capitalized value of its services, after taxes, and a capital gain on a house is effectively after-tax income for the same reason mentioned above for the value of a firm under our business tax.

Banks and Insurance Companies

Banks, insurance companies, and other businesses present a challenge to any tax system. Today, the practices of banks deprive the federal government of around $5 billion in revenue that the principles of the income tax ought to bring. Here is the problem: Suppose somebody has a balance of $100 in a personal account, averaged over the year. At market interest rates, he should earn at least $12 in interest, and this interest income would be taxable. But the bank clears a few dozen checks, issues 12 monthly statements, provides cash late at night from a machine, and delivers other services to the customer. Instead of sending him a bill for the price of these services, the bank deducts their price from his interest and pays him the difference, if any. In this example, there probably isn't any interest left over. The government is the loser, because the full interest income should have been taxed, and the cost of the services is not deductible. In effect, the customer has been allowed to deduct the cost of the bank's services, even though the cost would not be deductible if it were paid separately.

At first, it may seem that the simple tax would overcome this problem effortlessly. The interest the bank might pay the customer explicitly would not be taxed under our system. But the problem arises in another place—the application of the business tax to the bank itself. A bank that did nothing but maintain noninterest-bearing checking accounts for its customers, and invested the funds in bonds, would have no revenue on the top line of the business tax form—it would not appear to be selling any product to anybody. Its ample income from the bonds would be ignored. But it would have all the expenses for tellers, accountants, and servicemen for its cash machines, deductible under the business tax. It would appear to operate at a loss year after year. In practice, the loss would offset the many other activities of banks that generate actual revenue, and the government would be the loser in reduced revenue from the business tax. Banks are just as big a problem under the simple tax as they are today.

The answer is simple, and would apply today just as well as after tax reform. Banks should be prohibited from subtracting the price of financial services from interest payments. Instead, they should report market interest earnings on all accounts, and then subtract the price of the services explicitly. The top line of a bank's business tax return should include the full value of all the services provided to customers.

Here is the tax form that would have been filed by a typical medium-sized bank, the Old National Bank in Evansville, Indiana:

HALL-RABUSHKA SIMPLIFIED FLAT RATE TAX FORM

Form 2	Business Tax		1982
Business Name Old National Bank		**Employer Identification Number** 42-65226	
Street Address P.O. Box 718		**County** Vanderburgh	
City, State, and ZIP Code Evansville, Indiana 47705		**Principal Product** Banking Services	
1 Gross revenue from sales	**1**	34,979,324	
2 Allowable costs			
(a) Purchases of goods, services, and materials	**2(a)**	6,073,672	
(b) Wages, salaries, and pensions paid to employees.	**2(b)**	5,075,258	
(c) Purchases of capital equipment, structures, and land	**2(c)**	0	
3 Total allowable costs *(sum of lines 2(a), 2(b), 2(c)*	**3**	11,148,930	
4 Taxable income *(line 1 less line 3)*	**4**	23,830,394	
5 Tax *(19% of line 4)*.	**5**	4,527,775	
6 Carry-forward from 1981	**6**	0	
7 Interest on carry-forward *(14% of line 6)*	**7**	0	
8 Carry-forward into 1982 *(line 6 plus line 7)*	**8**	0	
9 Tax due *(line 5 less line 8, if positive)*	**9**	4,527,775	
10 Carry-forward to 1983 *(line 8 less line 5, if positive)*	**10**	0	

The bank's annual report for 1981, where we obtained these numbers, gives revenue from service charges and related fees of only about $4.5

million. But the bank's depositors maintained balances of over $350,000,000 during the year. Had they been paid market interest rates, they would have earned about $50,000,000. Instead, they received only about $20,000,000. The difference of about $30,000,000 is the market value of the services provided to the depositors by the bank, and appears along with the $4.5 million on line 1. One of the reasons the services have such a high value is government ceilings on deposit interest rates, which force small depositors to pay a stiff price for the safeguarding of their funds. After subtracting the bank's payroll and other allowable costs, taxable income on line 4 is a robust $23.8 million, on which the bank would have paid a tax of about $4.5 million. In fact, the Old National Bank paid no federal income tax at all in 1981. Even though the simple flat tax does not tax the interest receipts of banks, taxes would increase over their current level, which for the Old National Bank and many other banks is zero.

Taxation of life insurance companies should follow the same principle—they should be prohibited from netting the insurance premium against the return they pay on the cash value of a policy. Instead, they should pay market interest rates to policyholders and bill them for the full price of the insurance. Their income on the top line should be the total amount of premiums. Actual payments of claims are allowable expenses on the second line of an insurance company's business tax return.

The principle will be written into the law in a general way: under the business tax, interest paid to customers of any business may not be deducted from their purchases of the business's products.

Imports, Exports, and Multinational Business

We noted that the Exxon Corporation owns subsidiaries overseas. Should the U.S. government attempt to tax businesses owned by Americans, operating entirely outside the U.S.? Current tax law makes a pathetic attempt to tax them, but encounters an obvious problem. Businesses in other countries naturally pay taxes to those countries, and it is not realistic to extract much more tax for the U.S. Current law provides a generous credit for foreign taxes, whose effect is almost to eliminate taxation of overseas operations.

We favor the straightforward principle that the U.S. tax applies only to the domestic operations of all businesses, whether of domestic, foreign, or mixed ownership. Only the revenue from sales of products sold within the U.S. plus the value of products as they are exported is to be reported on the top line of the business tax form. Only the costs of labor, materials, and other inputs purchased in the U.S. or imported to the U.S. are allowable on the second line as deductions for the business tax. Physical presence in the U.S. is the simple rule that determines whether a purchase or sale is included in taxable revenue or allowable cost.

To see how the business tax would apply to foreign trade, consider first an importer selling its wares within the U.S. Its costs would include the actual amount it paid for its imports, valued as they entered the U.S.—this would generally be the actual amount paid for them in the country of their origin. Its revenue would be the actual receipts it obtained from sales in the U.S. Second, consider an exporter selling to foreigners goods produced in the U.S. Its costs are all of the inputs and compensation paid in the U.S., and its revenue is the amount received from sales to foreigners, provided that the firm did not add to the product after it departed the U.S. Third, consider a firm that sent parts to Mexico for assembly, and brought back the final product for sale in the U.S. The value of the parts as they left the U.S. would count as part of the revenue of the firm, and the value of the assembled product as it entered the U.S. would be an expense. The firm would not be allowed to deduct the costs of its Mexican assembly plant.

Under the principle of taxing only domestic activities, the U.S. tax system would mesh neatly with the tax systems of our major trading partners. If every nation used the simple tax and followed the principle, all income throughout the world would be taxed once and only once. Because the principle is already in use in the many nations with value added taxes, it makes sense for the U.S. to adopt it as well.

By the same principle, the compensation tax applies to the earnings of everyone working within the U.S., whether or not they are Americans, but does not apply to the foreign earnings of Americans.

Choices about the international location of businesses and employment are influenced by differences in tax rates. The U.S., with the low marginal rate of 19 percent, would be much the most attractive location among major industrial nations from the point of view of taxation. Although the simple tax does not tax the overseas earnings of American workers and businesses, there is no reason to fear a mass exodus of economic activity. On the contrary, the favorable tax climate in the U.S. would draw in new business from everywhere in the world.

CHAPTER 4

The Big Economic Issues

Tax reform along the lines of our simple tax will influence the American economy profoundly. Improved incentives for work, entrepreneurial activity, and capital formation will raise national output and the standard of living substantially. Everyone favors an economic renaissance. But what about some of the other effects of tax reform? Is it a giveaway to the rich? Will it destroy the housing market by ending mortgage deductions? Can charitable institutions survive without tax deductions for gifts? These are questions that have occurred to almost everybody pondering our radical reform, and they are questions we take seriously. This chapter tries to take an honest look at these major economic issues.

Incentives, Effort, and Growth

The simple tax is not immediately a good deal for most Americans. Unless the tax improves the performance of the economy, it will let a minority of high-income families off the hook for the very high taxes they are now paying and finance the move by slightly raising everybody else's taxes. Passage of the simple tax by majority vote makes sense only if the voters are persuaded, as we are, that the simple tax will bring the faltering American economy back to life. Voluntary submission of the majority to the simple tax is an investment that will pay off in future years in higher levels of well-being for every income group.

The great majority of economically active Americans would face improved incentives for productive effort under the simple tax. In 1979, married taxpayers had marginal rates under 18 percent only if their taxable income was less than $7600. The majority of families in that year had marginal tax rates of 24 percent or higher and just 19 percent had incomes so low or deductions so high that their marginal rates were below 18 percent. Even these figures understate the improvement in incentives, because many of the couples taxed at low rates are in school or are retired. Only 7 percent of total gross income was earned by couples taxed below 18 percent on the margin. Half of all gross income was taxed at marginal rates of 28 percent or higher. The net effect of equalizing marginal rates at 19 percent is a dramatic improvement of incentives for almost everybody who is economically active. All of our statements have been phrased in terms of married taxpayers because such a large fraction of single taxpayers are children or retired people with little likelihood of work or entrepreneurial effort and correspondingly low tax rates.

One point we need to get straight at the very start is that a family's marginal tax rate determines its incentives for all types of economic activity. There is much confusion on this point. For example, some authors have written that married women face a special disincentive because the marginal tax on the first dollar of their earnings is the same as the marginal tax on the last dollar of their husband's earnings. It is true that a woman with a well-paid husband has seriously eroded incentives to work because of high tax rates. But so does her husband. What matters for both of their decisions is how much of any extra dollar of earnings they keep after taxes. Under the U.S. income tax, with joint filing, the fraction either of them takes home after taxes is always the same, no matter how their earnings are split between them.

Sheer hours of work is one of the most important dimensions of productive effort, and one that is known to be sensitive to incentives. At first, it may seem difficult for people to alter the amount of work they supply to the economy. Aren't most jobs 40 hours a week, 52 weeks a year? It turns out that only a tiny fraction of the work force is restricted in that way. Most of us face genuine decisions about how much to work. Teenagers and young adults—in effect anybody before the responsibilities of parenthood—typically work much less than full time, full year. Improving their incentives could easily make them switch from part time to full time, or to spend less time taking it easy between jobs. But the simple tax would have its smallest influence in this group, whose many problems have little to do with the income tax.

Married women remain one of the largest underutilized resources in the U.S. economy, although a growing fraction enters the labor market each year. In 1981, only 65 percent of all women aged 25 to 54 were at work or looking for work; the remaining 35 percent were spending their time at home, but could be drawn into the market if the incentives were right. There is simply no doubt about the sensitivity of married women to economic incentives. Every study has shown a systematic tendency for women with low after-tax wages and high incomes from their husbands to work very little. Those with high after-tax wages and lower incomes work a lot. It is an altogether reasonable inference that sharply reduced marginal tax rates on married women's earnings will further stimulate their interest in the market.

Another remarkable source of wasted labor power in the U.S. is the early retirement of men. Though 94 percent of men aged 25 to 54 are in the labor force, only 71 percent of those from 55 to 64 are at work or looking for work, and just 18 percent of those over 65. Again, retirement is very much a matter of incentives. High marginal taxation of earnings discourages many perfectly fit men from continuing to work. Because mature men are among the best paid in the economy, a great many of them face marginal tax rates of 30, 40, or even 50 percent. Reduction to a uniform 19 percent could significantly reduce early retirement and make better use of the skills of older men.

An excellent study by MIT economist Jerry Hausman, published by the Brookings Institution, has measured the potential stimulus to work effort from tax reform. For a flat-rate plan quite similar to ours, he projects an increase in total hours of work in the U.S. economy of about 8 percent. A few workers would reduce their hours, either because the flat rate would exceed their current marginal rate, or because the reform would add so much to their income that they would feel that earning was less urgent. But the great majority would face much improved incentives. The increase of 8 percent would be about 3 hours per week on the average, but would take the form of second jobs for some workers, more weeks of work per year for others, as well as more hours per week for those working part time. The total annual output of goods and services in the U.S. economy would rise by about 6 percent, or almost $200 billion. That is nearly $1,000 per person—an astonishing sum. Of course, it might take some time for the full influence of improved incentives to have their effect. But Hausman's bottom line is unambiguous: tax reform would have an important favorable effect on total work effort.

Entrepreneurial Incentives and Effort

The U.S. economy has run out of steam in the past decade, and surely one of the reasons is the confiscatory taxation of successful endeavors and the tax subsidy for safe, nonentrepreneurial undertakings. There aren't any scholarly studies with quantitative conclusions on the overall benefits from a fundamental shift, but it could be large. Output per hour of work in the U.S. economy today is about 15 percent below where it would be if we had followed the growth trend of the 1950s and 1960s. From 1950 to 1973, it grew at a robust 2.8 percent per year; since 1973, its growth has been a meager 0.7 percent. The slowdown coincided with the perverse shift in tax incentives associated with the tremendous growth of government in the 1970s.

Today's tax system punishes entrepreneurs. Everything revolves around the leakage through interest deductions. The people in the driver's seat in the capital market, where money is loaned and borrowed, are those who lend out money on behalf of institutions and individuals who have figured out how to avoid paying income tax on their interest. These people don't like insecure loans to new businesses based on great new ideas. What they do like is lending secured by mortgages or similar arrangements to readily marketable assets. It's easy to borrow from a pension fund to build an apartment building, buy a boxcar, put up a shopping center, or anything else where the fund can foreclose and sell the asset in case the borrower defaults. Funds won't lend money to entrepreneurs with new ideas, because they are unable to evaluate what they could sell off in case of a default.

Entrepreneurs can and do raise money the hard way, by giving equity interests to investors. An active venture capital market operates for exactly this purpose. But the cost is high to the entrepreneur—the ownership he gives to the financial backers deprives him of the full gain in case things work out well.

So far we have just described the harsh reality of trying to get other people to put money into a risky innovative business. Even with the best tax system, or no taxes at all, entrepreneurs would not be able to borrow with ordinary bonds or loans and capture the entire future profits of a new business. Equity participation by investors is a fact of life. But it is the perverse tax system that much worsens the incentives for entrepreneurs. The combination of corporate and personal taxation of equity investments really is close to confiscatory. The owners of a successful new business are taxed first when the profits flow in, at 46 percent, and again when the returns make their way to the entrepreneur and the other owners. All of them are likely to be in the 50 percent bracket for the personal income tax. Even if they are clever enough to convert every bit of their earnings from the business into capital gains, taxed at 20 percent, the combined effective tax rate is close to 60 percent. The entrepreneur first gives a large piece of the action to the inactive owners, who put up the capital, and then well over half of the remainder to the government.

The prospective entrepreneur will likely have his attention diverted to the easier life of the investor who uses borrowed money. How much easier to put up a shopping center, borrow from a pension fund or insurance company, deduct everything paid to the inactive investor as interest, and sell out later for a capital gain taxed at only 20 percent. Many of these benefits are available even without any direct involvement—every issue of *The Wall Street Journal* has dozens of ads for purchase of cattle, real estate, medical equipment, and a variety of other investments eligible for financing through borrowing. Anybody in the upper-income tax brackets can be an accomplice in the diversion of effort and capital just by responding to one of these ads.

Today's absurd system taxes entrepreneurial success at 60 percent while it actually subsidizes leveraged investment. Our simple tax would put the same low rate on both activites. A huge redirection of national effort would follow. And the redirection could only be good for national income. There is nothing wrong with shopping centers, apartment buildings, airplanes, boxcars, medical equipment, and cattle, but the tax advantages have made us invest far too much in them, and their contribution to income is correspondingly low. Real growth will come when effort and capital flow back into innovation and the development of new businesses, where confiscatory taxation has discouraged investment, and the contribution to income from new resources is correspondingly high.

Total Potential Growth from Improved Incentives

Take Hausman's estimate of a 6 percent increase in output from increased total work in the U.S. economy. Take a modest additional increment to total output of 3 percent from dramatically improved entrepreneurial incentives. The sum of 9 percent is our best estimate of the improvement in real incomes after the economy has had 7 years to assimilate the changed economic conditions brought about by the simple flat tax. Both the amount and the timing are conservative; they do not remotely resemble the exaggerated claims of the supply-siders.

Even this limited claim for economic improvement represents enormous progress. By 1990, it means each American will have an income about $1400 higher, in 1982 dollars, as a consequence of tax reform. This economic dividend is more than enough to offset most of the adverse immediate effects of tax reform.

The Poor, the Middle Class, and the Rich

Now for some bad news. The simple tax does not make everybody better off straight away. Heavy taxation of successful people yields quite a bit of revenue, as well as pushing them out of their most productive undertakings and diverting their attention to tax avoidance. Until a response to improved incentives takes place, it is an obvious mathematical law that lower taxes on the successful will have to be made up by higher taxes on average people. If tax reform is a zero-sum process, giving relief to a minority by raising taxes on the majority, it is a political impossibility. Revitalization of the economy, with more income to divide between the big earners and the rest, is the point of tax reform. The 4 to 6 percent cut in income in the lower brackets brought about immediately by tax reform will soon be repaid by faster growth and higher incomes.

Because the critics of the flat tax have already made a big point about their calculations of who wins and who loses when taxes are reformed, we will spend some time on the issue. The first thing to say is that the critics are right on their own ground. If incomes remain exactly the same after tax reform, then the poor and the middle class subsidize the rich. Though all calculations of this kind are full of questions and uncertainties, no matter how we do it, we reach the same general conclusion. Tax reform is not immediately a good thing for the majority.

For the moment we will proceed as if tax reform had no effect on anyone's effort, though we emphatically do not accept that notion. Under this ground rule, some indisputable facts make it clear why improving incentives for the most successful Americans reduces the tax we extract from them. In 1979, 30 percent of all personal income tax revenue came from taxpayers who paid $10,000 or more in tax. These are high-income people—their gross incomes are $50,000 or above and their marginal tax rates are above 43 percent. Under the ground rule, where these people don't respond to lower tax rates, cutting the tax rate to 19 percent has to take a big chunk out of tax revenue.

We have made our own version of calculations of the effects of tax reform on various income groups; the details are in Appendix C in the back of the book. Because our reform makes use of the business tax to collect an important amount of revenue, calculations of losers and gainers has to include the business tax, and since the business tax supplants the existing corporate income tax, the calculations for today's tax system have to include the corporate tax. In a nutshell, we assume that each income group pays the corporate tax in proportion to its reported receipt of dividends, and that each group would pay the business tax partly in proportion to its receipt of wages and salaries (to take account of the taxation of fringe benefits under the business tax) and partly in proportion to its reported receipt of dividends (on the assumption that income from businesses is distributed approximately like dividends).

Our computations, like everybody else's, take a purely mechanical approach to the question of how taxes are distributed across income groups. We ask: How much individual or corporate tax is paid on the income reported by individuals now, and how much compensation and business tax would be paid on the same income after tax reform? We aren't equipped to calculate how much tax people *really* pay, in the sense of how their incomes would be different if there were no taxes, nor can we give a definitive answer to the most important question— how will after-tax incomes change when taxes are reformed?

With all these apologies and qualifications, here is what we get. Tax reform would raise taxes by 3 to 5 percent of income from the lowest income groups up to those with incomes of $21,000. Then the effect would gradually die out, so that families with incomes of around $60,000 would come out even. Then the truly successful get a better and better deal. Families with incomes around $130,000 receive tax breaks of about 7 percent of income, those with incomes of $700,000 get 10 percent, and the handful with incomes approaching $2,000,000 get 13 percent.

It's really important to understand why this apparently regressive move actually would put the economy ahead and why it deserves the support of the great majority who seem to lose, by these calculations. The high-income groups include two types—one alert and sensitive to taxes, and the other more passive. We guess that the alert group far outnumbers the passive group, but it is hard to pinpoint the alert group, because their tax-avoidance tricks make them inconspicuous in the tables. High marginal tax rates drive the alert group into all kinds of activites to escape taxation, and the whole economy suffers from this distortion. On the other hand, the high rates pick up a good deal of revenue from the passive group. It's a worthwhile trade to give up a good part of the revenue from the passive group in order to get the alert, sensitive group back into their most productive activities, but it comes at a cost in revenue.

If we are right that improved incentives will actually raise real incomes by 9 percent after 7 years, then it won't take too long for the taxpayers who lose at the outset to come out ahead. The worst immediate impact of the flat tax is to reduce after-tax income by 5 percent; as soon as the economy has grown by an extra 5 percent thanks to tax reform, those families will be back to where they were. As growth continues, they will ultimately come out at least 4 percent ahead.

Interest Rates

The simple tax would pull down interest rates immediately. High interest rates today are sustained partly by the income tax deduction for interest paid and the tax on interest earned. Much of the pain of high interest is ameliorated by the tax benefit, and part of the income from interest is taken away by the IRS. Borrowers tolerate high interest rates and lenders require them. The simple tax permits no deduction for interest paid and puts no tax on interest received. Interest payments throughout the economy will be flows of after-tax income, thanks to taxation of business income at the source.

With the simple tax, borrowers are no longer so tolerant of interest payments, and lenders are no longer concerned about taxes. The meeting of the minds in the credit market, where borrowing equals lending, will inevitably occur at a lower interest rate. Potentially, the fall could be spectacular. Much borrowing comes from corporations and wealthy individuals, who face marginal tax rates of 50 percent and above. On the other hand, the wealthy, almost by definition, are the big lenders in the economy. If every lender and every borrower were in the 50 percent bracket, simple logic shows that a tax reform eliminating deduction and taxation of interest would cut interest rates in half—for example, from 16 to 8 percent. But the leakage problem in the U.S. is so great that the actual drop in interest would be far short of this huge potential. So much lending comes from pension funds and other devices by which the well-to-do get their interest income under low tax rates that a drop of half would be impossible. Lenders taxed at low rates would be worse off if taxation were eliminated but interest rates fell by half. The meeting of the minds in an economy with lenders enjoying low marginal rates before reform would have to come at an interest rate well above half the prereform level. But the decline would be at least a fifth—say from 16 percent to 13 percent. Reform would bring a noticeable drop in interest rates.

One direct piece of evidence is available on this point. Municipal bonds yield interest not taxed under the federal income tax. Tax reform would make all bonds like tax-free municipals, so the current rates on municipals gives a hint about the level of all interest rates after reform. In 1982, municipals yielded about one-fifth less interest than comparable taxable bonds. But this is a conservative measure of the likely fall in interest rates after reform. Today, tax-free rates are kept high because there are so many opportunities to own taxable bonds in low-tax ways. Why own a bond from the City of Los Angeles paying 12 percent tax-free when you can create a personal pension fund and hold a Pacific Telephone bond paying 16 percent? Interest rates could easily fall to three-quarters of their present levels after tax reform; rates on tax-free securities would then fall a little as well.

High interest rates are widely noted as a symptom of the unsatisfactory state of the American economy. But the decline in interest rates brought about just by putting interest on an after-tax basis would not by itself pull the economy out of the doldrums. To U.S. Steel, contemplating borrowing to finance a modern plant, the attraction of lower rates would be offset by the cost of lost interest deductions. In fact, if tax rates on borrowers remained at 50 percent, and interest rates fell by less than half, effective borrowing costs would *rise*, and the outlook for investment in new plant and equipment would worsen.

The simple tax does much more than put interest on an after-tax basis. Taxes on corporations are to be slashed—to a uniform 19 percent from the double taxation of 46 percent corporate on top of up to 50 percent personal. And investment incentives are improved through first-year writeoff. All told, borrowing for investment purposes will become a better deal, and an investment boom will surely follow the enactment of the simple tax. As the boom develops, borrowing will rise and will tend to push up interest rates. In principle, interest rates could rise to their prereform levels, but only if the boom is vigorous. We can't be sure what will happen to interest rates after tax reform, but we can be sure that high interest, low investment stagnation will not persist. Either interest will fall or investment will take off.

As a safe working hypothesis, we will assume that interest rates fall in the year after tax reform by about a quarter, say from 16 to 12 percent. We assume a quiescent underlying economy, not perturbed by sudden shifts in monetary policy, government spending, or oil prices. Now, take a look at the borrowing decisions before and after reform. Before, an entrepreneur considers an investment yielding one million dollars a year in revenue, involving $800,000 in interest cost at 16 percent interest. The entrepreneur pays 50 percent tax on the net income of $200,000, giving him an after-tax flow of $100,000. After reform, he earns the same $1,000,000, pays $600,000 interest on the same principal at 12 percent. He pays 19 percent tax on the earnings, without deducting interest, for taxes of $190,000. His after-tax income is $1,000,000 − $600,000 − $190,000 = $210,000, well above the $100,000 before reform. Reform is to his advantage, and to the advantage of capital formation. What he loses from denied interest deduction he more than makes back from the lower tax rate.

How can it be that both the entrepreneur and the government come out ahead from the tax reform? They don't—there is one element missing from this accounting. Before the reform, the government collected some tax on the interest paid by the entrepreneur—potentially as much as half the $800,000, but as our stories about leakage make clear, the government is actually lucky to get a small fraction of that potential. Even so, it is probably enough to make the government lose money, on net, from the impact of tax reform on this project.

To summarize, the simple flat tax automatically lowers interest rates. Without an interest deduction, borrowers require lower costs. Without an interest tax, lenders are satisfied with lower payments. The simple flat tax has an important effect on interest rates. In this chapter we examine its impact on housing, a matter of great concern to almost everybody. In the next chapter, we describe the influence of tax reform on investment in plant and equipment, where interest rate effects are equally crucial.

Housing

Everyone who hears about the simple flat tax, with no deductions for interest, worries about its effect on the housing market. Won't the elimination of the deduction depress the prices of existing houses, further slow the already leaden pace of new housing construction, and impoverish the homeowner who can only afford a house because of its interest deductions? Our answer to all of these questions is no, but we freely concede that there is a significant issue here. Some people *would* suffer capital losses—generally the same people who enjoyed windfall gains from the unprecedented inflation of the 1970s.

In all but the long run, house prices are set by the demand for houses, because the supply can only change slowly. If tax reform increases the cost of carrying a house of a given value, then demand will fall and house prices will fall correspondingly. For this reason, we are going to look pretty intensively at what happens to carrying costs before and after tax reform.

If tax reform had no effects on interest rates, its adverse effect on carrying costs and house values would be a foregone conclusion. A $100,000 house with a $50,000 mortgage at 16 percent has interest costs of $8000 per year before deductions and $5600 after deductions for someone in the 30 percent tax bracket. The monthly carrying cost is $467. Take away the deductions, and the carrying cost jumps to $8000 per year or $667 per month. Inevitably, the prospective purchaser faced with this change would have to settle for a cheaper house. Collectively, the reluctance of purchasers would bring house prices down so that the buyers could afford the houses on the market.

As we stressed earlier, tax reform immediately lowers interest rates. And lower rates bring higher house prices, a point dramatically impressed on homeowners in the early 1980s when big increases in interest severely damped the housing market. The total effect of reform depends on the relative strengths of the contending forces—the value of the lost interest deduction against the value of lower interest. We have already indicated that there are good reasons to think interest rates would fall by about 4 percentage points—say from 16 to 12 percent for mortgages. The value of the lost deduction, on the other hand, depends on just what fraction of a house a prospective purchaser intends to finance. First-time home buyers typically, but not always, finance three-quarters or more of the price of a house. Some of them have family money or other wealth, and make larger down payments. Families moving up by selling existing houses generally plan much larger equity positions in their new houses. Perhaps a down payment of 50 percent is the average, so families are paying interest (and deducting) on $500 per thousand dollars of house.

A second determinant of the carrying cost is the value of the deduction, set by the marginal tax rate. Among homeowners, a marginal rate of 30 percent is typical, corresponding to a taxable income of $25,000. Interest carrying costs per thousand dollars of house are

$500 borrowed × 16 percent interest = $80 per year before taxes and $56 per year after taxes. When tax reform comes, the interest rate falls to 12 percent, and carrying costs are $500 × 12 percent = $60 per year before and after taxes. Tax reform puts this buyer behind by $4 per thousand dollars of house per year, or $400 per year for the $100,000 house.

If this $400 per year were the end of the story, it would bring a modest decline in house prices. But there is another factor we haven't touched on yet. The buyer's equity position—the down payment—must come from somewhere. By putting wealth into a house, the buyer sacrifices the return the wealth would have earned elsewhere. The alternative return from the equity in the house is another component of the carrying cost. Tax reform almost surely reduces that component. As just one example, take a prospective buyer who could put wealth into an untaxed retirement fund if he didn't put it into a house. The fund holds bonds; after reform, the interest rate on bonds would be perhaps 4 percentage points lower, and so the implicit cost of the equity would be lower by the same amount.

To take a conservative estimate, tax reform might lower the implicit cost of equity by one percentage point as interest rates fall. Then the carrying costs of the buyer's equity would decline by $500 × 1 percent = $5 per thousand dollars of house per year. Recall that the buyer has come out behind by $4 on the mortgage interest side. On net, tax reform would *lower* the carrying costs by $5 − $4 = $1 per thousand, or $100 per year for the $100,000 house. Then housing prices would actually rise under the impetus of tax reform.

We won't argue that tax reform will stimulate the housing market. But we do feel that the potential effects on house prices are small— small enough to be lost in the ups and downs of a volatile market. Basically, reform has two effects—to reduce interest rates and related costs of funds (and so to stimulate housing and other asset markets) and to deny interest deductions (and so to depress housing). To a reasonable approximation, these influences cancel each other out.

If tax reform sets off a rip-roaring investment boom, interest rates might rise in the years following the immediate drop at the time of the reform. During this period, when corporations were competing strongly with home buyers for available funds, house prices would lag behind an otherwise brisk economy. The same thing happened in the great investment boom of the late 1960s. But to get the strong economy and new jobs that go with an investment boom, minor disappointments in housing values would seem a reasonable price.

What about the construction industry? Will a slump in new housing accompany a tax reform that banishes interest deductions, as the industry fears? The fate of the industry depends intimately on the price of existing housing. Were tax reform to depress housing by raising carrying costs, the public's interest in new houses would fall in parallel with its diminished enthusiasm for existing houses. Because tax reform will *not* dramatically alter carrying costs in one direction or another, it will not enrich or impoverish the construction industry. Whether the industry can escape from its current oblivion is quite another matter. Only in the longer run can fundamental tax reform together with stable antiinflationary policy put the economy back on the track of growth and prosperity with normal levels of construction.

So far, we have looked at the way a prospective buyer might calculate what value of house he can afford. These calculations are the proximate determinants of house prices. But they have no bearing on the situation of an existing homeowner who has no intention of selling or buying. To the homeowner, the loss of the tax deduction can be pure grief. Two circumstances create exceptions. If the mortgage has a floating or variable interest rate, as a good fraction of mortgages made in the past few years do, then the lower interest rate following reform offsets part of the lost deduction. Second, if the mortgage was made recently at high rates, then the homeowner can refinance at the new lower rates brought by reform. Third, homeowners with mortgages made in 1973 and earlier don't lose very much when interest deductions end—their mortgages have such low interest payments, thanks to small principals and low interest rates, that loss of deductibility isn't terribly costly.

The sufferers are those who took large fixed-interest mortgages in the late 1970s at rates around 12 percent. They lose substantial deductions, and don't get anything back from automatic interest rate reductions or refinancing. They sustain a straightforward capital loss from the moment tax reform goes into effect. The capital loss is no different from those suffered by diverse groups throughout the economy in the ups and downs of the past decade. Think, for example, of the savers whose purchasing power fell by 20 percent or more from the inflation of the 1970s. For the mortgagees of the late 1970s, in fact, the capital loss from banishing interest deductions offsets a capital gain the same group received when interest rates rose sharply at the beginning of the 1980s.

The gainers from the change in the taxation of mortgage interest are the savings and loans and other thrift institutions who make the bulk of mortgages. With lower interest rates, their portfolios of mortgages (other than variable-rate mortgages and those refinanced by the homeowners) immediately jump in value. The mortgages have depressed market values today because they compete with new mortgages and bonds with higher interest payments. The capital gain offsets part of the huge capital losses threatening the solvency of the thrift industry.

Charitable Contributions

Deduction of contributions to worthy causes would be a thing of the past under our tax reform. Will the nation stop supporting its churches, hospitals, museums, and opera companies when the tax deduction disappears? We think not. But we should also be clear that incentives matter—the current tax system with high marginal rates and tax deductions provides inappropriately high incentives for some contributions. The immediate effect of tax reform will be a small decline in giving. Later, as the economy surges forward under the impetus of improved incentives for productive activity, giving will recover and likely exceed its current levels.

In 1979, total contributions from individuals and corporations to charitable causes in cash and voluntary work was about $94 billion. Of this, only $24 billion was deducted on tax returns. The great bulk of contributions were not even affected by the law permitting deduction. We can confidently expect the continuation of the $70 billion in contributions being made today without any special tax benefits. Further, the bulk of contributions is made today by people in modest tax brackets—less than $7 billion in contributions were deducted in 1979 by families with taxable incomes over $35,000. In this connection, it is important to understand that well over half of all cash contributions go to churches, and these gifts are generally from the middle of the income distribution.

Churches have nothing to fear from tax reform, and, like most people and institutions, would have much to gain from better economic conditions brought about by reform. In spite of their dominant position in gifts, churches are not the leaders in fighting tax reform that denies deductions. Instead, institutions serving the absolute economic and social elite—universities, symphonies, opera companies, ballets, museums—are protesting the loudest. No compelling case has ever been made that these worthy undertakings should be financed by anybody but their customers. A glance at the crowd in any of them will tell you that it is perverse to tax the typical American in order to subsidize the elite institutions. But granting tax deductions for gifts is precisely such a subsidy.

Tax reform will be a tremendous boon to the economic elite from the start. Removal of tax deductions from their favorite cultural activities is a reasonable price to pay. With substantially higher after-tax incomes among their customers as well as donors, the universities and other institutions will make up part or perhaps all of the ground they will lose when tax deductions disappear.

5 CHAPTER

Transition to the Flat Tax

Experts in the ways of Washington tell us that fundamental tax reform must be phased in gradually. Like a drinker who is so dependent on alcohol that his life would be threatened by abstinence, the economy couldn't take the shock of an immediate move to the simple flat tax. Instead, the harmful toxin of the current tax system should be withdrawn gradually, and the good new system brought in equally gradually. Or so the thinking goes. We disagree altogether with a phased changeover. In our view, the economy would benefit most from immediate adoption of the simple flat tax.

Not only do we prescribe the adoption of the simple tax cold turkey, we favor stripping away all the accumulated expectations of deductions and benefits from the existing tax system. In the main, these are two: unused depreciation and interest deductions, personal and business. We think it would be a mistake to put special grandfather clauses into our tax code to preserve these deductions. In the first place, such a move would destroy the simplicity of our tax system. A significant part of the popular appeal of our flat tax is its twin postcard tax returns—just putting in the additional lines for preserving old deductions would double their size. In the second place, loss of depreciation and interest deductions is just one of hundreds of losses and gains brought about by tax reform. It makes no sense to single out these two deductions because the flat tax compensates successful high-income individuals by lower tax rates and a better-performing economy in the future.

Depreciation Deductions

Existing law lets businesses deduct the cost of an investment on a declining schedule according to a formula that spans around 10 years for equipment and 25 years for buildings. No depreciation deductions are allowed for land or inventories. From the point of view of the investing business, multiyear depreciation deductions are not as attractive as the first-year writeoff prescribed in our tax reform. Eliminating depreciation deductions is no problem as far as future investments are concerned, because first-year writeoff is even better. But businesses may well protest the unexpected elimination of the unused depreciation deductions they thought they would be able to take on the plant and equipment they installed before the tax reform. Our proposal simply ends these deductions, without any direct compensation.

How much is at stake? In 1979, total depreciation deductions under the personal and corporate income taxes came to $180 billion. The value of future deductions was about $750 billion, measured as present discounted value with an interest rate of 12 percent. In other words, a bond paying out interest equal to the total flow of depreciation would have had a market value of $750 billion. At the corporate tax rate of 46 percent, the actual loss to business owners from eliminating depreciation would be 46 percent of $750 billion, or $345 billion, a hefty amount. However, because our tax reform would lower the tax rate to 19 percent, the loss would be a more manageable $142 billion.

Chapter 3 showed this loss would fall mainly on businesses in the doldrums with low current investment, and correspondingly low benefits from first-year writeoff for new investment, but large backlogs of capital still to be depreciated. Dynamic industries would find the deprivation of past depreciation more than offset by the advantages of first-year writeoff for new investment.

We stress that ending depreciation on existing investments has no effects on the incentive to make new investments. That incentive is much enhanced over the existing situation by the lowering of tax rates and the introduction of first-year writeoff.

Interest Deductions

Loss of interest deductions (and its counterpart, elimination of taxation of interest income) is one of the most conspicuous features of our tax reform. In the last chapter we reviewed its implications for interest rates in general and the housing market in particular. Here we will say a little more about the immediate winners and losers upon the adoption of the simple flat tax. A crucial point is that the denial of interest deductions goes hand in hand with the elimination of taxation of interest. The first without the second—a feature of several other purported tax reforms—would have serious adverse consequences. Parallel treatment of interest on the income and expenditure sides is a basic requirement of a sensible tax system.

For corporations as a group, taking interest out of both sides of the tax equation is a good thing. In 1979, corporations received $289 billion in interest and paid out $261 billion. The difference of $28 billion is the net interest income of corporations. That income is taxable under the current corporate income tax, but not under our simple flat tax. Overall, corporations will benefit when net interest income drops from the tax base. Naturally, some corporations do better than others. Manufacturing corporations paid out $20 billion in net interest in 1979, while financial and insurance corporations received $87 billion in net interest. As a general matter, corporations producing goods and services will sustain a small loss, which will pale against their trillions of dollars of total assets. Financial corporations will enjoy a comparable gain, part of which we offset by taxing the value of bank and insurance services currently concealed through the practice of paying below-market interest on deposits and insurance policies.

For individuals, the immediate tax consequences of dropping personal interest deductions and taxation of interest income is negligible overall. As we noted in Chapter 1, it is a stunning fact that interest declared as income is almost exactly the same as interest deducted. Again, what is true on the average is not necessarily true for each individual. The poor stand to gain from putting interest on an after-tax basis. At adjusted gross incomes of $4000 to $6000 per year, the typical taxpayer has ten times as much interest income as interest deductions (though both are small) and necessarily gains from the elimination of the taxation of net interest. All the way up to adjusted gross incomes of $18,000 (in 1979), net interest is positive and taxpayers gain from the reform. The middle of the income distribution— adjusted gross incomes from $18,000 to $50,000—is the region where interest deductions exceed interest income, and the removal of deductions more than outweighs the cessation of taxation. But even the single income group most seriously affected, those with gross incomes between $25,000 and $30,000, the actual dollar cost is small. The average taxpayer in this group has interest earnings of $943 and interest deductions of $1799, or net interest deductions of $856. At our tax rate of 19 percent, the lost deduction on $856 is only $163, or $14 per month.

It is hard to see why we should get terribly upset about a transition issue whose worst effect is $14 per month. What makes our elimination of interest deductions tolerable is coupling it with the elimination of taxation of interest income. Purported tax reforms that fail to net interest earnings against interest deductions could encounter much more serious transition problems, as well as bringing economic inefficiencies in the longer run.

One type of tax return—partnerships—does show much larger interest deductions than interest income. Net deductions in 1979 were $14 billion. Law firms and other businesses taking the partnership form are not typically big borrowers; essentially all the net deductions are taken by real estate partnerships. These tax shelters, based on assets eligible for leveraging, as we discussed in the last chapter, contribute to the excess investment in shopping centers, apartment buildings, and related projects. Obviously the people involved in these shelters will squawk loudly when interest deductions are taken away. But they are mostly wealthy people, and should readily handle the disappointment. To protect them from the sudden imposition of a tax reform that eliminates a much-abused shelter does not, in our opinion, rest on firm social grounds.

Interest Rates, Investment, and Output

It is hard to predict the precise behavior of the economy during the transition to the simple flat tax. We are sure that the new tax is good for economic growth—it will stimulate the supply of productive effort through dramatically improved incentives and will stimulate the demand for output by raising real incomes and by improving the climate for investment. Moreover, as investment surges, the stock of productive plant and equipment will expand and the supply of output will grow on that account as well. The timing of the investment boom and the corresponding behavior of interest rates is more of a question. The overselling of supply-side economics at the outset of the Reagan administration makes us cautious about claiming too much for the immediate effects of tax reform.

The main point we want to make is that tax reform must produce either an investment boom or much lower interest rates. Unless improved investment incentives bring in a whole new set of borrowers to put new upward pressure on interest rates, the removal of tax deductions on one side and interest taxation on the other simply has to depress interest rates. Borrowers and lenders will take account of the changed taxation of interest and will agree to loans at an interest rate several percentage points lower than when interest was taxed and deducted.

There is no more hazardous occupation in economics than forecasting the performance of the U.S. economy, but we do want to illustrate some of the alternatives facing the economy. None of the numbers come out of an elaborate mathematical analysis of the American economy; instead, they simply represent our judgment about different ways the economy might evolve. First, here is a projection of the way things might develop in the absence of tax reform:

Year	Real GNP growth	Investment ratio	Prime rate
1983	2.0%	10.5%	11%
1984	4.0	11.0	11
1985	3.0	10.5	10
1986-90	3.0	10.5	10

Real GNP growth is the percent change in one year over the previous year in the economy's total output of goods and services, adjusted for inflation. The investment ratio is the amount of nonresidential investment expressed as a fraction of GNP. The prime rate is the short-term interest rate banks charge their most reliable customers. Basically, we foresee real GNP growth of around 3 percent, which means that the low level of activity in the economy, and consequent high unemployment, will continue for the rest of the decade, though modest growth will resume. Investment will be a little below its normal relation to total output. Interest rates will be well below their peaks of 1980 to 1982, but will remain at historically high levels. In essence, we, along with most other commentators, see the continuation of unsatisfactory conditions, but without a severe depression.

Tax reform will brighten the picture. The very significant improvements in investment incentives provided by the new business tax will stimulate the demand for investment goods directly, and other goods and services indirectly. Equally important improvements in the incentives for work and entrepreneurial effort will stimulate the supply side of the economy. Real GNP will grow more briskly and reach a notably higher level by the end of the decade. During the transition to the higher level, as we have stressed earlier, one of two things will happen—either investment will boom or interest rates will fall dramatically. Here is the way the picture might change if the investment boom followed quickly upon enactment of the simple tax:

Year	Real GNP growth	Investment ratio	Prime rate
1983	3.0%	11.0%	10%
1984	5.0	11.5	10
1985	5.0	11.5	9
1986	4.5	11.3	9
1987	4.5	11.1	8
1988	4.0	10.9	7
1989	3.5	10.5	7
1990	3.0	10.5	7

Real GNP growth is a percentage point higher in the first two years, then is two percentage points higher, and finally falls back to the same rate of growth by 1990, all compared to our earlier projection for the current tax system. By the end of the seven years, the level of real GNP and real income would be higher under the new tax system by about 9 percent. Even though increased *growth* would come to an end by 1990, the permanently higher *level* of output and income would confer a significant lasting benefit upon every American. Without tax reform, we project that GNP in 1990 will be about $16,600 per person in 1982 dollars. With the simple flat tax, that figure will be just over $18,000. Tax reform raises the productive output of the average citizen by over $1400. As we noted in the last chapter, the extra real income from tax reform more than offsets the tax increases imposed on low- and middle-income taxpayers.

In our projection for a speedy investment response, the interest rate falls as soon as the new tax is in place, but by only one percentage point relative to the earlier projection—the prime rate in 1983 is 10 percent with tax reform and 11 percent without. Increased demand for funds from new investment would limit the fall in interest rates brought about by taxing business income at the source. In later years, after the investment boom has run its course and investment is back down to its normal level of 10.5 percent of GNP, the prime rate will fall by its full potential amount. The prime rate in 1990 is 10 percent without tax reform and 7 percent with reform.

Another possibility is a much slower investment boom:

Year	Real GNP growth	Investment ratio	Prime rate
1983	2.2%	10.6%	9%
1984	4.3	11.3	10
1985	4.8	11.4	10
1986	5.0	11.5	9
1987	5.0	11.4	8
1988	4.4	11.0	7
1989	3.8	10.5	7
1990	3.0	10.5	7

In this projection, real GNP growth accelerates less in the first two years, but high growth lasts longer, compared to the previous projection. The total increase in the level of output by 1990 is the same 9 percent as in the case of a quick investment boom. The differences in the two projections of the effects of tax reform are in the timing, not the magnitude of the total response. Because investment is not putting as much pressure on credit markets in 1983, interest rates are lower in that year: 9 percent for tax reform with a slow investment response, 10 percent for reform with a quick response, and 11 percent with no reform and no investment response. By 1990, the prime rate is down to the same 7 percent as in the earlier case.

These projections will no doubt be falsified by the time they appear in print. We have included them to clarify the different forms the economic transition to the simple tax might take. All kinds of economic events, favorable and unfavorable, will perturb the economy during the 1980s; since we don't know what they will be, we can't include them in these projections. Still, we feel on firm ground in asserting that improved incentives for investment, work effort, and entrepreneurial activities will substantially raise real output, real incomes, and employment, and will significantly lower interest rates. Though 9 percent is our best guess about the overall increase in real GNP over the seven years, obviously it could be somewhat more or somewhat less.

Balancing the Budget

Sooner or later, the federal government will have to face up to the requirement of a balanced budget. Though experts—including the two authors of this book—disagree on the political and economic desirability of a budget in balance in each year, the government cannot operate with a large chronic deficit without serious adverse consequences to the economy and the society. Such a deficit means that part of the government debt will never be repaid, and if the public perceives that irresponsiblity, it will be increasingly reluctant to hold government debt. A functioning government debt market means the public believes that ultimately the budget will be balanced.

Would the simple tax help move to a balanced federal budget? The answer is a clear yes, for two reasons. First, the 19 percent tax rate would generate more revenue than the existing tax system even with the same level of economic activity. Second, tax reform would stimulate activity, and so generate increased revenue on that account as well.

We will start by comparing the revenue yielded by the simple 19 percent tax with the revenue from the existing personal and corporate taxes, at the same levels of economic activity. This comparison is highly conservative, since we are confident that the simple tax would stimulate activity and bring some underground enterprises to the surface. Computations of deficits involve a number of assumptions about the economy and the government; these are spelled out in detail in Appendix D. We have taken optimistic and pessimistic paths of overall economic activity (which affects the revenue from either the current tax system or the simple tax), government spending, and interest rates. The optimistic case adopts the forecast of economic activity and federal spending of President Reagan's 1983 budget message, while the pessimistic case follows an analysis made at the same time by the Congressional Budget Office. The results are:

DEFICIT, BILLIONS OF DOLLARS

Year	Current tax		Simple tax	
	Optimistic	Pessimistic	Optimistic	Pessimistic
1983	$91	$157	$51	$101
1984	83	188	29	102
1985	72	208	8	97

In all years and under both optimistic and pessimistic assumptions, the simple flat tax reduces the federal deficit by a large margin. In the optimistic case, the defict is $40 to $60 billion smaller, and in 1985, the federal budget is essentially in balance. Even with the pessimistic assumptions, the simple flat tax pulls the deficit down to a more manageable figure of around $100 billion from the alarming levels projected for the existing tax system.

These figures illustrate a point about the simple flat tax of central political importance: It is possible to reduce tax *rates* dramatically and yet raise revenue and close the deficit at the same time. Further, our computations so far do not consider any supply-side effects—everything comes from the enormous enlargement of the tax base accomplished by the simple flat tax.

The stimulus to investment and productive activity from the simple tax will raise income and so raise the revenue generated by the tax over the figures we just gave. How large might that effect be by 1985? Enough to make another important contribution to eliminating the deficit:

DEFICIT WITH THE SIMPLE TAX, BILLIONS OF DOLLARS

Year	Optimistic		Pessimistic	
	No response	Response	No response	Response
1983	$51	$47	$101	$97
1984	29	18	102	91
1985	8	−17	97	72

The figures for no response are the same as in the previous calculations. The figures for a response of GNP take the extra GNP growth from the quick investment response projections in the previous section. In the first year, 1983, one extra percent of GNP yields about $4 billion in added federal revenue. As growth accelerates and higher levels of GNP cumulate, the addition to federal revenue becomes more significant. By 1985, under the optimistic assumptions combined with the extra growth stimulated by tax reform, the federal budget swings into surplus for the first time since 1969. Even these computations are conservative in one respect—they do not include any allowance for the decline in interest rates brought about by reduced federal deficits.

Some Concluding Thoughts on the Transition

We have argued throughout this book that four principles should guide the design of a sound, sensible tax system. All are, in our view, equally important. We place as high a premium on simplicity as we do on low rates, or taxing all income only once, or exempting poor people from income taxes. Simplification promises fairness and renewed respect for the lawful obligation of Americans to pay their taxes. Simplification promises to arrest the growing disrespect and cheating on taxes that threaten the ability of the Internal Revenue Service to collect the revenue essential to pay for government activities. It also promises to save taxpayers billions of dollars.

We readily acknowledge that a shift from the present system to the simple tax would create another set of winners and losers. After all, each of the nine major postwar tax reforms has created shifting groups of winners and losers. In the aggregate, the effect of constant change has been to damage the economy and create hundreds of vested interests enjoying a multitude of exemptions, exclusions, deductions, and credits. By adopting the simple flat tax, we end once and for all the annual lottery of Congressional tax writing and worry over whether some groups gain and others lose. We eliminate the uncertainty by installing a tax system that is unlikely to need reform in the future. It is not too high a price to pay for the benefits of the simple tax if some holders of current benefits lose and some new winners emerge. The simple tax will be a durable reform, and no further rearrangement of tax burdens would be needed in the future.

If we were to phase in the simple tax gradually, every special interest would seek grandfather clauses or postponement of the loss of benefits as long as possible. Even if only a few of these interests succeed in hanging on to their special provisions, the flat tax will lose its essential simplicity. Furthermore, it will be difficult for the political process to grant preferential treatment to one special interest, and not hundreds of others. Whatever the appeal of any single group for special treatment, we dare not run the risk of complication and departure from the basic principles of sound taxation. Adoption of the simple flat tax in its starkest form is the best political course.

6

Questions and Answers about the Low, Simple, Flat Tax

We have spent a good deal of time presenting the simple flat tax and answering questions about it on radio talk shows, before professional and lay audiences, and testifying before Congress. In this chapter, we have assembled a number of the questions that have recurred in those discussions together with our answers. Many aspects of the simple flat tax are perhaps best explained in the question-and-answer form.

Deductions

Q: *What about charitable deductions?*

A: No charitable deductions would be allowed under the simple income tax. We do not believe that current tax incentives are a major part of the motivation to make contributions to community, religious, and other organizations that qualify for deductions at present. A large volume of contributions are made by people who cannot deduct the contributions because they do not itemize deductions. Deductibility of contributions is widely abused by wealthy taxpayers to avoid taxes. On net, you will save more by blocking the tax-avoiding tricks of the wealthy than you lose from the elimination of tax deductions from your own contributions. There is little merit in public subsidy for organizations whose success in raising funds depends on tax deductibility rather than the intrinsic merit of their activities.

Q: *What would happen to the restaurant industry?*

A: Though business meals are an important element of the restaurant industry, there is no reason to expect that the simple tax would reduce restaurant patronage. Neither the existing tax system nor the simple tax give business an incentive to spend money at restaurants rather than anywhere else. All reasonable business expenses, including restaurant meals, are deductible under either tax system. A limited amount of restaurant spending may arise from abuse of the current system by providing untaxed income to employees. This problem would be alleviated under a tax system with lower marginal rates. On the other hand, as the new tax system brings businesses out of the underground economy and into the market, taxed economy, spending at restaurants will be slightly increased. Neither effect should be large. The restaurant industry also stands to gain from the incentive effects of lower taxation of many of its employees.

Q: *Shouldn't the tax system provide some relief to families with high medical costs?*

A: Virtually the entire U.S. population is now covered by medical insurance, Medicare, or medical benefits through welfare. The medical deduction under the current personal income tax is a source of many abuses, including the deduction of swimming pools and other home improvements as medical expenses. Few families would suffer, and the overwhelming majority would gain, by closing off this source of abuse.

Q: *Why is there no deduction for moving costs in the simple tax?*

A: Moving costs are only one of hundreds of costs incurred by taxpayers in order to earn an income. It is inconsistent to permit deduction of moving costs when costs of commuting, purchase of special clothing, and other employment costs cannot be deducted. Many moves are undertaken for reasons unrelated to earning a higher income and so should not escape taxation. The deduction for moving expenses is one of a number of tax provisions abused by a small minority of taxpayers at the expense of the great majority. It should be eliminated.

Q: *I am a salaried employee. How would I treat unreimbursed business expenses? There is no room for this deduction on the simple individual compensation tax form.*

A: Deduction of so-called business expenses of salaried employees is a major loophole in the current tax system. It is widely abused to subsidize summer travel for teachers, trips to conventions, and other activities for which special incentives are inappropriate. Genuine business expenses ought to be borne by employers, in which case they are deductible under the business tax.

Q: *The current income tax grants deductions for certain adoption expenses. Do you want children to remain orphans to save a few dollars in government revenue?*

A: Deduction of adoption expenses is a good example of a well-intentioned complication of the tax system with little practical impact. Lower-income families can't take the deduction in many cases, and even if they could, it would have little importance because their marginal tax rates are not very high. All the benefits of the deduction go to prosperous families who do not need help from the government. By adding slightly to the financial attraction of adoption, the government only further increases the demand for adoptable babies, which already far exceeds the supply.

Housing

Q: *What would happen to the housing market as a result of ending the deduction for mortage interest?*

A: The simple tax would end the deduction for interest of all kinds, not just mortgage interest. It would not discriminate against housing. However, improvements in the taxation of business investment would tend to draw wealth out of housing and into plant and equipment, which might reduce housing values temporarily. The effect would not be more than a few percent, and would last only for the duration of the investment boom set off by the new tax system. In the longer run, the outlook for housing values would be improved as overall economic activity increased in response to the tax.

Q: *How would the flat tax affect the savings and loans, who are in so much trouble today?*

A: Like all owners of long-term debt, savings and loans would receive a benefit from the lower interest rates brought about by the flat tax. The market value of their mortgages would rise as interest rates fell, improving their currently depressed net worth. Because the interest the savings and loans would pay on their borrowing would fall, their operating deficits would decline.

Q: *Why shouldn't we tax the capital gain from the sale of a house?*

A: These capital gains are rarely taxed under the current system, because of the rollover provision, forgiveness of capital gains for the elderly, and the stepping up of the basis for capital gains at the time of inheritance. We believe that the taxation of housing is properly ceded to local governments under the federal system. Local property taxes capture part of the value of the services of a house. A capital gain occurs when the market valuation of the services rises. These gains arise from after-tax income, just as capital gains from the ownership of business arise from after-tax income. Hence taxation of capital gains would amount to double taxation.

Q: *The only way I can afford my house today is the large tax deduction I get for the interest on my mortgage. Won't I have to sell my house if I can no longer take the deduction?*

A: Don't overlook the benefits you will receive from a much lower tax rate. Suppose you and your husband earn $60,000 per year and pay $18,000 in mortgage interest. Your tax in 1981 would be $11,553, after taking account of the large deduction for interest. Under the simple tax, you would not be able to take the deduction—your tax would be 19 percent of $55,000, or $10,450. You come out more than a thousand dollars ahead, even though you can no longer take the deduction. If you could afford your house before, you can certainly afford it now. However, if you have been extremely aggressive in taking advantage of interest deductions, so you are paying little tax in spite of a large income, you will come out behind with the simple tax.

Q: *I plan to install solar heating in my house and know the current tax law offers a credit for this energy conservation investment. Will I still receive this tax credit under the simple tax? If not, won't this discourage conservation and make us wasteful of energy?*

A: Like all the complications of the existing tax system, the residential energy credit would disappear with the advent of the simple flat tax. The energy credit makes little economic sense—it puts the taxpayers' money into elaborate installations which are at or below the margin of economic efficiency. With all forms of energy except natural gas already decontrolled, and gas decontrol on the way in the later

1980s, homeowners face the right incentives for solar energy investments without any special tax gimmicks.

**Q: *Since your plan removes the tax incentives now offered for
preservation of historic structures, won't this accelerate the de-
struction of many buildings that belong to our national heritage
and should be saved for future generations to enjoy?***

A: For every genuinely important historical building saved by the
tax incentives, dozens or perhaps even hundreds of buildings are subsidized that are not important or would be kept by their owners anyway.
Accelerated depreciation for historical structures is a terribly inefficient
way to accomplish the goal of preservation—most of its effect is to
create yet another tax shelter. Direct appropriation of local government
funds for saving individual buildings is far superior as a social policy
for preservation.

**Q: *Doesn't the simple tax encourage speculation in land by
granting first-year writeoff for land purchases?***

A: The sellers of land have to count their proceeds as taxable
income; this offsets the deduction granted to the purchaser. Prices of
undeveloped nonresidential land may rise a little, but with a 19 percent
tax rate, this effect should be very small. Land transactions are included
in the simple tax because it is very difficult to separate the value of
land from the value of buildings on it.

Intergovernmental Relations

**Q: *How would local governments be affected by the change in
the taxation of bonds?***

A: Local governments derive a small advantage from the tax-free
status of their bonds and the taxation of all competing bonds in the
current system. Under the simple tax, local government bonds would
remain untaxed, but all other bonds would also provide tax-free interest, because the earnings of business would be taxed at the source.
The immediate impact of the simple tax would lower the borrowing
costs of other borrowers to the levels paid by local governments. In
the ensuing investment boom, as interest rates rose, local borrowing
costs would gradually rise. The slightly adverse effect on local governments would be confined to a few years, and would not be large.
In the longer run, local governments would face no higher interest

rates and would benefit in many other ways from the improved performance of the U.S. economy.

**Q: *What about such other taxes as state, county, excise, and
sales taxes? What would happen to them under the simple income
tax?***

A: Although we would prefer that other government units besides
the federal government switch to taxes based on the same principle as
the simple income tax, we have limited our proposal to federal action.
The only important implication of our proposal for other taxes is the
elimination of the deduction for other taxes under the federal personal
income tax. Because this deduction is important only for higher-income
families, who benefit enormously from lower marginal tax rates, we
do not believe that the elimination deduction will have any harmful
effects. Elimination of the tax deduction promotes efficiency by removing the incentive to channel economic activity through state and
local governments.

**Q: *How would the simple income tax affect state taxes where
the tax returns are linked to the federal tax system?***

A: Because the new federal taxes would raise approximately the
same revenue as the old taxes, a state that retained the linkage would
continue to receive about the same revenue as well.

**Q: *How does the simple tax treat government? Are state and
local activities taxed? Does the federal government tax itself?***

A: State and local governments pay no taxes themselves, but their
employees pay the compensation tax on their wages, salaries, and
pensions. Similarly, the federal government does not tax itself, but its
employees pay the compensation tax.

Retirement

**Q: *How are existing IRA and Keogh retirement accounts treated
under the simple tax?***

A: IRA and Keogh accounts have provided benefits to a limited
fraction of taxpayers of the same type that the simple tax would provide
to all taxpayers. Under the simple tax, they would be treated exactly
as under the current system, except that the tax rate would usually be
much lower. When the accounts begin to pay retirement benefits, those

benefits would be taxed as compensation. It would no longer be necessary to impose a minimum age for the payment of benefits. Holders of IRA and Keogh accounts could elect to liquidate their accounts at any time, and pay the compensation tax at that time. For the future, IRA and Keogh accounts would not be necessary, because the taxation of interest income at the business rather than the personal level would give any form of savings the same advantage as IRAs and Keoghs have today.

Q: *Interest on the savings in my life insurance policy is excluded from current taxation under today's law. What will happen to the life insurance industry and the value of my insurance when taxation of all interest is eliminated?*

A: As far as you are concerned, the tax benefits you are enjoying will continue—there will be no taxes on the interest you are earning. Furthermore, when your insurance pays off, you will not have to pay income tax on the interest component, as you do under current law. As far as the industry is concerned, taxation of its interest earnings and deduction of its interest payments will end. Only its actual insurance premiums will count as income, not the saving that goes with some types of insurance, and only its payoff for death and other insured events will count as business expenses.

Business and the Rich

Q: *Isn't the simple tax a windfall to the rich?*

A: Taxation of families with high incomes and few deductions would be dramatically reduced under the simple tax. On the other hand, taxes paid by those who take advantage of the almost unlimited scope for reducing or postponing taxes through tax shelters and other gimmicks will rise a great deal. The simple tax would be a windfall to the hard workers and a loss to those who have concentrated on avoiding tax.

Q: *Is the simple tax progressive?*

A: The simple tax is progressive in the sense that families with higher incomes pay a larger fraction of their incomes in taxes. Families with incomes below the personal allowance level pay no tax at all. The proportion of income paid in tax rises to close to 19 percent for the highest income. Proportions of income paid as tax are:

Income	Tax
$10,000	4.4%
15,000	9.2
20,000	11.7
30,000	14.1
40,000	15.2
50,000	16.1

Q: *Does business pay its fair share of taxes under the simple tax?*

A: Only people pay taxes. The simple tax is designed so that income from business sources is taxed at the same rate as income from employment. Under the current system, some business income is taxed at excessive rates because of the double taxation of corporate dividends. Other business income is lightly taxed or even subsidized through tax shelters.

Q: *Isn't the tax unfair because rich people can live off interest and capital gains income and thereby pay no taxes?*

A: Not at all. In effect, the simple tax puts the equivalent of a withholding tax on interest and capital gains. The business tax applies to business income before it is paid out as interest, or if it is retained in the business and generates capital gains for stockholders. The interest, dividends, and capital gains received by the rich have already been taxed under the business tax. The rich cannot escape the tax.

Q: *Won't part of the tax on capital be shifted onto consumers in the form of higher prices rather than being paid by the owners of the capital? Isn't this unfair relative to the compensation tax, which will not be shifted?*

A: Yes. There is a fundamental difference between capital, which is a produced input, and labor, which is a primary, unproduced input to the economy. Because it permits first-year writeoff of investment, the simple tax puts no tax on the marginal addition to capital—the tax benefit of the writeoff in the first year just counterbalances the taxes that will be paid from its productivity in the future. For this reason, the tax is not actually shifted forward. On the other hand, all of the growth in the revenue from the simple tax comes from growth in the size and real incomes of workers. It is not an issue of equity but rather of economic reality that all taxes bear fundamentally on labor income.

The simple tax embodies the right incentives for people to save labor income to form capital.

Q: Isn't it unfair not to tax capital gains received by individuals?

A: Capital gains *are* taxed under the simple tax. Capital gains from the sale of a business property—an office or an apartment building, or a house held for investment purposes—would be taxed under the business tax, which treats the proceeds from the sale of plant, equipment, and buildings as taxable income for the business. Capital gains on stocks, bonds, and other financial instruments arise from the capitalization of after-tax income; it would be double taxation to tax the capital gain as well. Capital gains on owner-occupied houses arise from the capitalization of rental values which are heavily taxed by state and local governments; again, it would be double taxation for the federal government to tax the capital gain as well.

Q: Why does the simple tax collect the business tax from the firm and the compensation tax from the worker? Wouldn't it be more consistent to collect both from the firm or both from the individual?

A: The nation's experience in trying to collect income taxes on interest and dividends from individuals has been dismal. One of the huge advantages of the flat-rate simple tax is that it permits airtight collection of taxes on business income at the source, where enforcement is easiest. On the other hand, requiring individuals to fill out the compensation form is necessary to provide the benefits of the personal allowance to each taxpayer. The tax withholding system already in operation would be adapted to permit the collection of most of the compensation tax from the employer, so that taxpayers would not be faced with a large single tax payment at the end of the year.

The Business Tax

Q: What would happen to the unused depreciation deductions from capital investments made under the old tax system?

A: These deductions would simply be lost. In the first place, much lower tax rates make the deductions much less important—reduced taxation of the earnings of capital completely offsets the decline in the value of the deductions because of lower tax rates. In the second place, the existing combination of an investment credit taken at the time of purchase and accelerated depreciation for tax purposes means that most plant and equipment has already received most of the tax benefits; eliminating the remaining depreciation would not impose an important burden on business.

Q: *I'm a traveling salesman. I earn commissions and pay my own travel expenses. I do not receive a salary. How would I fill out the simple tax?*

A: All self-employed individuals will file the business tax form, where they can deduct business expenses. In order to take advantage of the personal allowance, you will want to pay yourself a salary of at least, say, $6200 if you are married. Report this amount along with your wife's earnings on your compensation tax form. In this way, you will be able to deduct your legitimate business expenses and receive the personal allowance.

Q: *Please explain how the current system taxes income twice. Isn't income income no matter what its source?*

A: Income is an individual's command over resources. Only people have income. The income of a corporation is just the income of its owners, the stockholders. The current tax system sometimes taxes the same income twice, once when the corporation receives it and again when it is paid as dividends to the stockholders. The combined tax rate on the stockholder's income is almost confiscatory, even though the two separate taxes are at rates of around 50 percent.

Q: *How are tax losses for individuals and businesses treated?*

A: Remember that the self-employed fill out the business tax form just as a large corporation does. Business losses can be carried forward without limit to offset future profits. There is no such thing as a tax loss under the compensation tax. You can't reduce your compensation tax by generating business losses.

Q: *Would a company going bankrupt get a tax refund in proportion to its loss?*

A: No. The simple tax would never make payments to taxpayers. However, a bankrupt company could be acquired by another firm, which would assume the tax loss.

Q: *Some companies pay so much interest today that requiring them to pay the business tax (which does not permit the deduction of interest) would make them operate at a loss. Is this appropriate?*

A: This is an aspect of the transition to the simple tax. Corporations and homeowners with large amounts of debt will suffer, just as those with large holdings of bonds or mortgages will gain. For two reasons, the problem will not be too serious. First, the dramatic reduction in the tax rate to 19 percent will more than offset the increase in taxes from the loss of interest deductions in most cases. Second, most corporate debt can be called and reissued at lower rates as soon as the simple tax goes into effect.

Q: *If a firm plowed back all of its income into plant and equipment, and hence paid no business tax, couldn't the firm increase its value forever without paying taxes? Wouldn't the stockholders receive the capitalized value of the firm as untaxed capital gains?*

A: Sooner or later, the firm will run out of sufficiently profitable opportunities and will start paying out its income to its owners instead of plowing it all back. If the market didn't believe this, the stock would have no value, because the stockholders would not believe that they were ever going to get anything. The market will always know that the tax will be imposed on any returns earned by the stockholders, so the market value of the firm will always be the capitalized value after taxes.

Q: *Won't businesses constantly buy and sell equipment in order to take advantage of the immediate writeoff?*

A: There is nothing to be gained from extra purchases and sales. The proceeds of a sale of equipment must be reported as income, and offset the tax benefits of a subsequent purchase.

Q: *How are individuals taxed on their rental activities? Is rental income part of individual compensation or business income? Would individuals have to file both business and individual tax forms if they had both kinds of income?*

A: Renting is definitely a business activity and would call for a business tax form. Rental receipts are taxed as business income, but purchase of a rental unit qualifies for first-year writeoff. Because there are no complicated depreciation computations, very little effort would be required to fill out the business tax form for a rental unit.

Q: *If a company provides its employees with subsidized lunches, physical exercise facilities, company cars, and the like, how are these treated under the simple tax?*

A: Fringe benefits cannot be deducted as expenses under the business tax. Of the firm's expenditures for the purpose of attracting and keeping workers, only those paid directly to the worker and reported for the purposes of the individual compensation tax are deductible by the company.

Q: *As an investor, I currently find that percentage depletion is better than cost depletion for my oil wells. What will happen to depletion under the simple flat tax?*

A: Depletion will disappear as a special complication of the tax law. Instead, first-year writeoff will apply to all purchases of oil property and all development costs.

Q: *I am involved in a highly leveraged investment company. Won't my company and others like it be forced out of business by the simple tax because we won't be able to deduct interest expenses any more?*

A: It is true that you will no longer be able to deduct interest expenses. But it is likely that your borrowing is linked to market interest rates. If so, the decline in interest rates upon the adoption of the simple tax will offset the loss of the deduction. Also, don't forget that the income from your company will be taxed at only 19 percent. Try filling out the business tax return to see what will happen to your total tax payment.

Q: *Does the simple tax cover the fringe benefits of government and nonprofit organizations?*

A: Yes. They are required to file the business return in a particular way that exempts all of their income except what is paid to their employees as fringes. In this way, the simple tax avoids a distortion in favor of government and nonprofit activities which would arise if they alone could pay untaxed fringes.

Q: *How will the simple tax affect the value of the U.S. dollar in the foreign exchange market?*

Q: The tax treatment of imports and exports of goods and services will be essentially the same under the simple tax as under the existing income tax, so there will be no change in the value of the dollar on that account. The lower interest rates that will accompany tax reform may bring a temporary decline in the value of the dollar, which will stimulate U.S. exports and discourage imports.

The Compensation Tax

Q: *With the current income tax, my fringe benefits aren't taxed. Your simple tax doesn't tax fringes either, but it does not permit my employer to deduct them. What will happen to my fringe benefits under the simple tax?*

A: Your fringe benefits are one of the features that attracted you to your job, and your employer will not want to cut them without compensating you in some other way. The simple tax eliminates the distortion toward fringe benefits created by the present income tax, so you can expect that your employer will offer you reduced fringes in exchange for higher pay, which you can use to buy the benefits yourself or for any other purpose.

Q: *My teenage daughter has taken a part-time job and will earn about $1000 this year. Can she use the personal allowance of $3800 to avoid paying tax? Will I lose my dependent's allowance of $750 for her?*

A: All taxpayers are entitled to the personal allowance, including your daughter. You will retain the dependent's allowance as long as you provide more than half her total support over the year.

Q: *As a member of the armed forces, I get to exclude certain benefits and allowances from my pay for tax purposes. What will happen under the simple tax?*

A: The benefits you receive in kind—for example, military housing—are not taxed under the individual compensation tax. Just like a private employer, the Defense Department will have to pay the Treasury a business tax on the value of those benefits. Your cash benefits will be taxed under the individual compensation tax. The government will have to make a modest increase in these cash benefits in order to offset the 19 percent tax you will have to start paying on them.

Q: *I am an American citizen and now enjoy a $75,000 exclusion for income earned abroad. How will this income be treated under the simple flat tax?*

A: All income earned from work performed abroad, or from enterprises located abroad, is excluded from the simple tax. Such income will be taxed by the country where you earn it.

Q: *The simple flat tax eliminates the credit for child and dependent care expenses. Won't this force people to stay home to take care of their children and elderly dependents, thereby increasing their dependence on welfare, reducing their participation in the labor force, and cost the government more money than it would save from its elimination?*

A: Like many of the complications in the tax system, the child care credit fails to focus its benefits in an area of particular social need. In effect, it lowers the taxes of a significant fraction of all taxpayers—families with two earners and one or more children. It is available at all income levels. Higher tax rates are required to finance this lowering of the amount of taxes. Features like the child care credit are antithetical to the flat-tax philosophy, which favors a broad tax with the lowest tax rate. We think that the special problems of helping poor families with child care and other responsibilities should be attacked specifically within the welfare system, not with the scatter gun of the tax system. The simple flat tax provides plenty of revenue for a generous welfare program.

Q: *Isn't it unfair to start taxing workman's compensation?*

A: Workman's compensation makes payments to replace wages when a worker is disabled on the job. The wages themselves would have been taxed, so it stands to reason that the replacement should be taxed. Failing to tax workman's compensation would create an inappropriate incentive for workers to remain off the job after a period of disability.

Q: *Why does the simple tax eliminate the extra exemptions for the blind and the elderly? What makes you want to lay higher taxes on these two especially unfortunate groups in our society?*

A: Many of the elderly and a few of the blind are quite well off. It raises everybody's tax rate inappropriately to provide extra exemptions to every elderly and blind individual. It makes sense to concentrate policies with respect to the incomes of the elderly in the social security system—the value of the current extra exemption is trivial compared to the social security benefits received by the typical older person. For the blind, efforts should be concentrated in welfare agencies, not in the tax system.

Q: *Part of my compensation comes in the form of stock options. How are these taxed?*

A: The full market value of the options is included in your compensation in the year you receive them, whether or not you exercise them.

Non-profit Organizations

Q: *How does the simple tax treat nonprofit organizations like cooperatives that pay dividends?*

A: They are exempt from the business tax, but their employees must pay the individual compensation tax. As under present law, their dividends are untaxed. Note that nonprofit organizations cannot benefit from the investment incentive of first-year writeoff either.

Q: *What about nonbusiness entities such as trusts, estates, or charitable organizations including churches and schools?*

A: Any actual business owned by one of these entities must file the business tax form. Their employees must pay the individual compensation tax. Otherwise, they are not taxed. Note that a conventional personal trust, which holds stocks and bonds, deals entirely in after-tax income and there is no reason for the tax system to pay attention to it.

Inheritance

Q: *What about the inheritance tax?*

A: We do not believe that an inheritance tax is necessary under a ystem with watertight comprehensive taxation of income.

Q: *Wouldn't it be a good idea to broaden the tax base by including gifts, life insurance proceeds, inheritances, and so forth?*

A: No. The base for the simple tax is carefully chosen to provide the most efficient economic incentives. Further broadening to the listed items would be double taxation. Gifts represent the transfer of income that has already been taxed and there is no reason to tax it again. Life insurance proceeds are a mixture of interest earnings, which have already been taxed by the business tax, and return of premiums, which again were paid from income already taxed. Inheritances are just a special form of gifts.

Economic and Social Benefits

Q: *How will the simple tax change the spending and savings patterns of individuals and businesses?*

A: The improved, uniform investment and savings incentives provided by universal first-year writeoffs will channel capital into its most productive uses. Equalization of tax rates across taxpayers will prevent the widespread abuse of tax shelters that divert savings from their efficient destinations. Dramatic reductions in marginal tax rates will stimulate investment and work effort, and draw activities out of the underground economy and into the more efficient market economy.

Q: *How much time and money will we save by having to fill out only the two postcard returns in place of Form 1040 and all its schedules?*

A: The Treasury estimates that businesses and the public spend over 600 million hours filling out returns; almost all of this would be eliminated by the simple tax. At a conservative value of $6 per hour, that 600 million hours is worth $3.6 billion.

Q: *It sounds like the simple flat tax is just a clever ploy to raise taxes on the already overburdened American taxpayer. Aren't we actually better off with the present system, with all its defects?*

A: It is true that many people's taxes will rise a little right after the tax reform. But quickly everyone will benefit from the increased economy activity that will accompany a dramatic improvement in the incentives facing the most critical participants in our economy. Within seven years, we foresee a 9 percent increase in real incomes on account of the simple tax, almost double its immediate tax increase for any income group.

Q: *How will the simple tax help the American economy to grow?*

A: The most obvious and best-documented effect comes from workers' response to improved incentives. With lower tax rates, the take-home pay from extra work—longer hours, more weeks per year, or a second job—will rise. For the most productive and highly paid workers, taxed today at rates up to 50 percent, the improvement in work incentives will be especially dramatic when their tax rate falls to 19 percent. More subtle, but equally important sources of growth will come from the vast improvement in the incentives for entrepreneurial activity. Today's tax system puts tax rates as high as 60 or even 70 percent on the rewards to successful innovation, thanks to the cascading of the corporate and personal income taxes. With the taxes rationalized by the new business tax, at the low rate of 19 percent, bright people will be attracted to innovation and away from the tax-sheltered activities favored by the current tax system. Finally, the simple tax provides stronger incentives for capital formation, an important source of growth in the longer run.

Q: *What will happen to the stock market when the simple flat tax goes into effect?*

A: As a general matter, the market will not respond very strongly, though some companies may experience important changes in their market valuation. Lower tax rates and the elimination of the taxation of dividends will tend to raise the market. On the other hand, the loss of deductions for interest and depreciation on existing plant and equipment will depress the market. In the longer run, the effects will be positive, as the favorable incentive effect begins to dominate.

Q: *What about the international value of the dollar?*

A: Enactment of the simple flat tax would depress interest rates in the U.S. To an extent that would depend on the monetary and fiscal policies of other major nations, world interest rates would fall in tandem. If world rates are allowed to fall by less than U.S. rates, the dollar would depreciate relative to other currencies. In the longer run, interest rates around the world will tend to equalize, and the effects of the tax reform on exchange rates will disappear.

CHAPTER 7

Comparing Flat-Tax Proposals

In 1982, Congress began considering no less than a baker's dozen flat-tax bills. Some bills went through the IRS code, systematically repealing or amending it section by section. Some stated basic principles of a flat tax and instructed the Treasury to draft the appropriate technical language to implement their guidelines. Some only requested the Treasury to conduct a feasibility study of the flat-rate concept, and report alternative flat-tax systems to Congress in six months' time.

The several plans encompassed in these bills vary enormously. One set imposes a uniform flat rate. Another involves tax schedules that are not really flat, but begin with a "normal" rate, then apply a surcharge to successively higher brackets of income, following the tradition of the original 1913 Income Tax Act. Some plans only reform the personal income tax; others both the personal and corporate income taxes. Every plan grants an exemption in the form of either a personal allowance or a tax credit. Most proposals eliminate all other deductions; a few keep the most popular ones intact—for example, home mortgage interest. Most of the bills aim at collecting the same amount of revenue as the current tax system.

There is a good deal of apprehension and confusion about the flat tax and what it will do to the economy and the countless ways in which people in different economic, business, and tax circumstances will be affected. Part of this concern arises because stories about the flat tax often oversimplify or leave out details of specific plans. For example, many commentators portray the flat tax as eliminating all deductions, including business expenses. It makes a world of difference whether business depreciation is eliminated or replaced by a 100 percent investment writeoff in the first year. Similarly, stories may suggest that the flat tax eliminates personal allowances, thereby imposing alarming new taxes on the poor. In fact, a personal allowance or credit is a feature of every current proposal. Scaremongering has frightened homeowners, charitable organizations, and other special interest groups that have a big stake in the existing structure of deductions.

To address and put to rest many of these worries, we have explained at length our fully integrated flat-tax proposal (embodied in Senator Dennis DeConcini's bill, S. 2147) and how it would affect the performance of the economy and different groups of taxpayers. At this point, it is useful to evaluate the other proposals which have been offered to see how they stack up against ours. We hope to persuade you that ours is the most thoroughly thought-out, comprehensive plan.

How to Evaluate Flat Tax Plans

By now it should be abundantly clear that a low-rate income tax must tap a broad base of national income. This, in turn, requires sealing the leakage in the current system. Tax cheating must become uneconomic, undesirable, and harder to get away with. Participants in the underground economy must find it more attractive to surface. Finally, individuals and firms must be guided in their actions by the rewards of earning higher incomes (and keeping 81¢ of each dollar),rather than saving taxes (now often 50¢ on each dollar).

Recall the four rules on which our plan rests.

1. All income should be taxed only once, as close as possible to its source.
2. All income should be taxed at the same low rate.
3. The poorest should pay no income tax.
4. The tax forms for businesses and individuals should be simple enough to fit on postcards.

Our plan, faithful to all four principles, captures income that now slips through the tax net, at the same time ending double and triple taxation of interest and dividends. When business income is taxed at its source, it is possible to design an administratively simple, efficient system to collect business-generated taxes from a much smaller number of businesses than from the hundred-plus million individuals to whom business now pays some of its earnings for subsequent taxation. The Hall-Rabushka plan taxes all national income, other than investment and personal allowances. In so doing, a greatly enlarged taxable base of income allows a low flat rate to generate sufficient federal revenue.

Our second rule is equally crucial to the success of any flat tax. First, it would be a misnomer to call a plan with multiple rates or surcharges a flat tax. Graduated rates, by any other name, are still graduated rates. Second, unless all income is taxed at the same rate, people will use any means they can find or concoct to shift taxable income from higher to lower tax brackets, by assigning income to their children, for example. But it is also impossible to collect taxes on dividends and interest income at the source unless all taxpayers are taxed at the same rate, because we cannot know in advance the correct tax bracket of each recipient, and therefore do not know how much to withhold. We can only put interest and dividend income on an after-tax basis when a single rate is applied.

That the poorest should pay no tax, our third guideline, is guaranteed in the form of a generous personal allowance. A secondary effect of a personal allowance is to make of our plan a progressive tax system; the higher your income, the more of it you pay in taxes. The principle of exempting the poorest is so uncontroversial that every flat-tax proposal thus far includes either a personal allowance or individual credit.

A fourth, but not least, guideline is simplicity. The flat-tax movement enjoys grass-roots support largely from its promise to substitute a postcard for Form 1040 and its accompanying booklet of bewildering instructions. Since December 10, 1981, our correspondence has repeatedly stressed the importance of simplicity coupled with the certainty that the rich would have to pay a fixed 19 percent share of their income in taxes that the most clever lawyers could not circumvent. The knowledge that special deductions, shelters, and breaks available only to the rich would be eliminated means a great deal to ordinary middle-class Americans, even if some rich people pay less taxes in our system. Two postcard-sized forms replace the entire panoply of short and long Forms 1040, corporate returns, small business returns, and so forth. Some 400 million bits of reported interest and dividends paid to individuals would be eliminated. So too some 100 million Forms 1099. And these are but two tips of an iceberg.

Few scholars today quarrel that current tax policy harms capital formation and economic activity. Adopting a single, low flat-rate tax would restore incentives to work, save, and invest. In truth, we could call economic growth a fifth criteria of tax reform. Chapter 4 shows how our plan stimulates the economy, leading to an overall improvement in the standard of living.

A Catalog of Flat-Tax Proposals

All flat-rate tax plans introduced in 1982 can be divided into five categories.

1. Requests for Treasury studies.
2. A gross income tax on business receipts.
3. A 10 percent flat tax on personal income, with no provision for changing current corporate taxation.
4. A 19 percent flat tax on personal income, with provisions for low rates on corporate income.
5. Graduated rates on personal income, with a flat-rate tax on corporate income, or no change in current corporate taxation.

The first two categories are easy to summarize. On tax-return day (April 15, 1982), Senator Charles Grassley of Iowa introduced S. 2376, which directs the secretary of the treasury to study the feasibility of replacing the current income tax code for individuals and corporations with a flat-rate or a reduced progressive (fewer and less steeply graduated rates) system, levied on an enlarged base of income. Four possible broader measures of income include gross income, consumption, a percentage of consumption, or just paring down many of the loopholes in the current code.

A second measure is Texas's Lloyd Bentsen's Senate Joint Resolution 206, which calls on the secretary of the treasury to review and propose for the consideration of the Senate Finance Committee at least three alternative federal income tax systems containing flat-rate structures. In the *Congressional Record* preceding the resolution (page S. 7498), he cites, among others, the studies of Hoover Institution experts.

The third request for a Treasury study closely parallels that of Senator Grassley. Introduced on March 17, 1982, by Representative Kent Hance of Texas, H.R. 5868 directs the secretary of the treasury to conduct an in-depth study of a low-rate, gross income tax system along the lines developed by Mr. Jim Jones of Blanco, Texas. GIT, the acronym for gross income tax, proposes a single-rate tax on the gross receipts of every business entity, without allowing any deductions for the costs the firm incurred to produce its revenues. GIT would force firms with losses to pay the same tax on its receipts as firms with profits.

Category three consists of three 10 percent and one 15 percent flat-rate plans. The 15 percent plan was introduced by Idaho's Congressman George Hansen on October 22, 1981, as part of a broader goal of taxpayer protection in limiting the collection excesses of the IRS. H.R. 4821, amended by Mr. Hansen on April 26, 1982, specifies a 13 percent flat rate on personal income, estates, and trusts, maintaining religious giving as the sole lawful deduction. It includes a $3,000 personal exemption for a couple, with $1,000 per dependent. An additional 2 percent rate is also included to retire the national debt. For corporations, Hansen's bill imposes a flat 14 percent charge on gross receipts minus business deductions.

The three 10 percent measures evince, at times explicitly, the historical doctrine of the tithe. In modern times, the state has replaced the church as the chief collector of revenue. Republican Philip Crane of Illinois introduced H.R. 5513 on February 10, 1982. It provides for a 10 percent rate on personal income, and repeals all deductions, credits, and exclusions, other than a $2,000 deduction for each person. The bill contains no provision for corporate taxation, leaving the current code in place.

Ron Paul of Texas introduced a companion bill in the House on May 11, 1982 (H.R. 6352). Paul differs from Crane to the extent that he would give an exemption of $10,000 to individuals. Paul also explicitly acknowledges that his plan would reduce revenue.

Over on the Senate side, the 10 percent rate has been introduced by North Carolina's Jesse Helms. (S. 2200 was thrown in the bill hopper on March 15, 1982). In his statement, Helms cites the studies of Alvin Rabushka and Robert E. Hall of the Hoover Institution to justify his contention that a low, flat-rate income tax can raise as much revenue as the current system. Helms states that he is not formally committed to the 10 percent rate except as a reasonable starting point from which to debate tax reform. On the religious point, Helms invoked the same phrase Phil Crane had earlier used in the House, that "Caesar should ask no more" than the tithe of his earnings man owes to God. Neither Helms nor Crane modify the corporate income tax. Before moving to the fourth category, the 19 percent look-alike plans, we might note that none of the 10 percent plans solve the problems of leakage that riddle the current system.

The fourth category consists of 19 percent plans. Apart from our plan, Senator Dennis DeConcini's bill (March 1, 1982), California's Leon Panetta, H.R. 6070 (April 5, 1982), and Tennessee's John Duncan, H.R. 6303 (May 6, 1982), introduced virtually identical bills. They tax gross income of individuals, estates, and trusts at 19 percent, giving a credit against taxes of $1,000 for the taxpayer, $1,000 for a spouse, and $200 per dependent, with an additional $200 credit for the aged and blind. All other deductions, exclusions, and credits are eliminated. On the corporate side, they tax the first $50,000 of business profits at 3 percent, rising at 3 percent increments every additional $50,000, to a maximum 15 percent rate on corporate profits over $200,000. Though Panetta does not cite our research papers in his opening statement, the text reads with remarkable familiarity. Selection of a 19 percent rate seems more than mere coincidence. The one apparent difference lies in the use of a personal credit in place of our personal allowance, though this substitution is not important.

Despite the identical 19 percent rate, important differences separate our plan from the Panetta-Duncan approach. In our attempt to tax all income as close as possible to its source, we have redefined the business tax to include much of the professional, interest, dividend, proprietorship, farm, rental, and royalty income that today falls under the personal income tax. This novel feature curtails leakage and eliminates a good deal of the administrative and reporting complexity of the current code. Panetta-Duncan still retain these types of business income under the personal income tax and keep the existing corporate tax, but at a lower rate. They thereby double-tax corporate income at rates approaching 31 percent, not including taxes from capital gains in the stock market. Nor can we discern the logic of a graduated rate scale for corporations. A 15 percent maximum corporate rate is an incentive for individuals to incorporate in a 19 percent world, especially if the retirement and other benefits of incorporation under current law continue.

While Duncan and Panetta greatly simplify reporting requirements and record-keeping, we would be hard pressed to design a postcard or one-page form for their plan. Space would be needed to report interest, dividends, rents, royalties, farm income, capital gains, and so on. Individuals, rather than business firms, would continue to be the collection points for income taxes on these sources of income. We are not gainsaying their progress in simplification and lowering marginal rates; however, to the extent that leakage is not plugged, the measures would be self-defeating. Under their system, a 19 percent rate would not raise sufficient revenue for the government.

The fifth and final category is not true flat-rate proposals, but rather simplified multiple-rate schemes. The Senate Record of May 20, 1982, contains the text and statement preceding Dan Quayle's S. 2557. In his statement, Indiana's Senator Quayle specifically documents the Hall-Rabushka plan, citing its 19 percent flat rate. But Quayle goes on to advocate ''retaining at least some progressivity in the tax structure.'' He uses the word progressivity to mean graduation in the rates.

S. 2557 would grant each taxable individual an exemption of $17,500, impose an 18 percent rate on taxable incomes from $17,500 to $50,000 and a 7 percent surcharge, or a 25 percent rate, on incomes beyond $50,000. Corporate profits would be assessed at 20 percent.

Quayle would broaden the definition of taxable income to include unemployment insurance, employers' contributions to health benefits, credits for child care expenses, food stamp benefits, and so forth. Quayle has also read our proposal carefully, for he would not tax dividends, interest, and capital gains at the individual level, noting that such income has already been taxed via the business tax. He would permit a capital recovery allowance in plant and equipment investment, but does not spell out the timetable for depreciation.

The last, and to date the most publicized flat-tax plan is that of Senator Bill Bradley of New Jersey and Congressman Richard Gephardt of Missouri, jointly introduced in both Houses of Congress on August 5, 1982 (S. 2817/ H.R. 6944). The seeming popularity of this plan with the public, the press, and its quasi-official blessing at the Democratic Party's midterm summer convention force us to devote special consideration to it. From our viewpoint, the plan is replete with flaws that requires massive changes. Otherwise, adoption of Bradley-Gephardt is just another tinkering job with the current code.

The Bradley-Gephardt Proposal

To begin with, Bradley-Gephardt is not a flat tax. It shrinks the number of tax brackets from 15 levels to four, and limits the allowable deductions to a chosen handful. Senator Bill Bradley and Representative Richard Gephardt have entered their streamlined reform measure into the flat tax sweepstakes and have enjoyed vastly more attention than all the other plans rolled together. What are the main features of their proposal?

In a press release dated May 27, 1982, Senator Bradley acknowledges numerous problems with the existing tax code. It is, he says, "too complex as a result of repeated attempts to use it as a vehicle for political favoritism and social engineering. Even lawyers and accountants often cannot make sense out of the maze of deductions, exclusions and credits in the code." As well, high tax rates limit incentives to work more, to save more, and to invest more—the language of a true supply-sider. Tax preferences encourage people to allocate resources inefficiently, driven more by the tax than productive consequences of their decisions. Finally, the public perceives the system as unfair. To correct these problems, Senator Bradley advocates lowering tax rates and broadening the tax base.

Bradley and Gephardt call their plan a "Comprehensive Individual Income Tax Proposal." Their bill itself is 47 pages long. It does not in any way address the corporate income tax. It rests on the current concepts of taxable income and adjusted gross income (AGI) we find on pages 1 and 2 of Form 1040. It includes all those kinds of unincorporated business income now assigned to individual tax returns. They levy a basic tax rate of 14 percent on taxable incomes below an AGI of $25,000 for single returns and below an AGI of $40,000 for joint returns. To this is added a progressive surtax imposed on total income (defined as AGI) in three stages reaching 14 percent, for a combined tax rate of 28 percent above $37,000 AGI for single returns and $65,000 AGI for joint. The complete rate schedules are as follows:

SINGLE RETURNS

Adjusted Gross Income	Surtax Rate	Combined Tax Rate (Surtax plus 14% basic tax)
Below $25,000	None	14%
$25,001–$30,000	6%	20%
$30,001–$37,000	11%	25%
Over $37,000	14%	28%

JOINT RETURNS

Adjusted Gross Income	Surtax Rate	Combined Tax Rate (Surtax plus 14% basic rate)
Below $40,000	No tax	14%
$40,001–$55,000	6%	20%
$55,001–$65,000	11%	25%
Over $65,000	14%	28%

Bradley and Gephardt retain the following provisions in the Internal Revenue Code:

- The zero bracket amount, which would be increased from $3,400 to $4,600 for joint returns.
- The taxpayer exemption, which would be increased from $1,000 to $1,500 for single returns; from $2,000 to $3,000 for joint

returns; and from $1,000 to $1,750 for single heads of household. Each additional exemption is worth $1,000.

Combining the zero bracket and taxpayer exemption creates a personal allowance of $7,600 for joint returns, and $4,900 for single.

The 1982 personal income tax contains 12 graduated tax brackets ranging from a low of 12 percent to a high of 50 percent. For 1984, the number of brackets would rise to 14, and tax rates would stretch from 11 to 50 percent. Bradley-Gephardt collapses the 1984 rate band from 14 brackets to 4, simultaneously reducing the top marginal rate from 50 to 28 percent—a cut in the top marginal rate of 22 percentage points. For most taxpayers, it lowers the top marginal rate, since the standard 14 percent rate holds until AGI of $40,000 on joint returns. Under current law, someone in the $40,000 bracket would pay a 1984 marginal rate of 33 percent.

Bradley-Gephardt retains the most popular deductions in the current code:

- employee business expenses
- home mortgage interest
- charitable contributions
- state and local income taxes and real property taxes
- exclusion for social security and veterans' benefits
- exemption of interest on general obligation bonds.

Modifications to present law include plans to convert the child care credit to a deduction, reduce by one-third the exclusion for employer-provided health insurance, reduce the amount of exclusion for sale of elderly-owned homes, limit medical deductions to expenses in excess of 10 percent of AGI, and apply a 14 percent tax on the investment income of pension, IRA, and Keogh plans.

To broaden the tax base, they propose repeal of 26 provisions in the current code. A sample includes the current exclusion for income earned abroad by U.S. citizens or residents, the exclusions for interest and dividends (thus raising taxes on interest and dividends), the 60 percent deduction on long-term capital gains (thus raising capital gains taxes from the current maximum 20 percent to a new maximum 28 percent rate), the exclusion for unemployment compensation benefits, the regular investment tax credit, among others. In the process, 26 entries are expunged from the tax forms.

In their press release, the two members of Congress construct nine hypothetical taxpayers to show that 80 percent of all taxpayers would pay no more than the standard rate of 14 percent; only 20 percent would be subject to the surtax. They estimate that taxpayers claiming the standard deduction would pay less due to the lower rates; those claiming few itemized deductions would pay about the same; those with significant deductions, credits, and exclusions would pay more on average. Redistributing the tax burden this way has a strong populist appeal, promising 60 to 70 percent of taxpayers lower and simpler taxes, while increasing taxes on the upper 30 to 40 percent of the population.

What's Wrong with Bradley-Gephardt?

The best way to look at any proposal for tax reform is to apply the four criteria we have consistently used to develop and evaluate the flat-rate tax. Rule one is to tax all income once and only once, as close as possible to its source. On this criterion, Bradley-Gephardt offers only modest improvement. By repealing 26 current deductions, some leakage in potentially taxable income is plugged. However, serious cracks remain.

Taxation of interest and dividend income will not change, thereby continuing to be double taxed, first at the corporate level and then again when received by individuals. Nor will the large sums of interest and dividend income that go unreported necessarily get reported.

So long as income from interest, dividends, rents, royalties, capital gains, professional activities, and farming is taxed at the individual level, as it will be in their plan, underreporting will persist. The only successful way to fully tax such income is to tax it at its business source.

Another problem area is the retention of a handful of existing deductions, in particular, those for home mortgage interest, charitable contributions, state and local taxes, and general obligation bonds. In 1979, the dollar value of these four deductions exceeded $130 billion. 1982 totals range from $180 to $200 billion, which substantially erodes the base of taxable income. Unless Bradley and Gephardt successfully contain the lawful deductions to just the six they have selected, we would expect further erosion in their tax base as pressure is applied to reinstate all of the other equally meritorious 26 deductions they have selectively repealed.

The second guideline to sensible tax reform is to tax all income at the same low rate. We have shown how people shift income from high-bracket to low-bracket family members. This ploy is but one of many that rich people exploit to pay lower tax rates on chunks of their income.

We think it unwise to retain a deduction for home mortgage interest. Again, the deduction conflicts with the principle of putting interest on an after-tax basis. Under Bradley-Gephardt, its retention discriminates against low-income and in favor of high-income households. Why? Because families in the standard 14 percent rate zone only save 14 cents on each dollar of mortgage interest, compared with 28 cents on the dollar for those paying the top surtax. This pattern of discrimination applies to all deductions, including charitable donations and tax-exempt bonds. A counterpart to taxing high incomes at unequal rates is to reward deductions at unequal rates.

A key word in the second principle is *low*, taxing all income at the same *low* rate. Low rates of taxation are a linchpin of strong economic growth and greater investment, savings, and work effort. Indeed, Senator Bradley prefaced his announcement of May 27, 1982, with supply- side language of restoring incentives to work more, save more, and invest more. In the same breath, though, he proposed a substantial increase in capital gains tax rates, from 20 to 28 percent— damaging the incentives our equity markets require. Since Bradley and Gephardt claim that 60–70 percent of all taxpayers, who are situated in current tax brackets below 33 percent, would pay less, they acknowledge that the remaining 30–40 percent would have to pay higher taxes to sustain current revenue. Raising taxes on the upper third of taxpayers belies Bradley's supply-side rhetoric. His hope is that many taxpayers would willingly give up their current tax preferences and time spent trying to avoid or reduce taxes in exchange for lower marginal rates. Still, a tax increase on the most productive part of our population, coupled with a higher levy on venture capital, are not a recipe for renewed economic growth.

The third rule of tax reform is that very poor people should pay no federal income taxes. On this score, Bradley-Gephardt compare favorably with other flat-tax proposals. Combining the personal exemption and zero bracket exempts married couples from taxes on the first $7,600 of their income; for single persons, the figure is $4,900. These levels discharge the poorest members in our society from the burden of paying federal income taxes.

Exemptions and the zero bracket bring about a progressive system, even *without* graduated surtax rates. However, Senator Bradley describes his proposal as an improvement of the current system rather than a radically different kind of tax, and seeks progressivity through both a generous personal allowance *and* a graduated rate structure.

The fourth principle of tax reform is simplicity. Bradley and Gephardt simplify the tax forms, the steps needed to compute taxes, and the amount of record-keeping required to substantiate tax returns. By no stretch of the imagination, however, would the Bradley-Gephardt taxpayer be able to file his return on the back of a postcard. Indeed, taking the current Form 1040, he would need to fill out much of pages 1 and 2, Schedule A for the retained itemized deductions, B for interest and dividend income, C for business income, D for capital gains, E for rents and royalties, and so on. Redrawing Form 1040 to conform with Bradley-Gephardt would disclose that true simplicity eludes their grasp.

It is worth dwelling for a moment on some economic effects of the Bradley-Gephardt plan. Retaining mortgage deductions distorts the way Americans spend their money by continuing a major source of leakage. When the time comes for legislation, the hundreds of vested interests that have grown up around the preferences in the tax code will argue that their special case is just as deserving as a house purchase, or charitable giving, or tax-exempt bonds, or? or? or? All the while, deducting mortgage interest and other items shrinks the tax base, forcing marginal rates higher.

It makes no economic sense to limit interest deductions just to home mortgages. Cars, consumer durables, college tuition, vacation travel, investment in stocks, and other spending can enjoy the same benefit under Bradley-Gephardt. How? Simply by increasing the size of your mortgage, using the money for investment or consumption, and deducting the interest costs. Those in the 28 percent range will find such behavior twice as rewarding as the great bulk who pay only 14 percent.

Bradley-Gephardt also contains one very worrisome political feature. By taxing 80 percent of the voters at the standard 14 percent rate, and the remaining 20 percent at rates up to 28 percent, it creates incentives for Congress to impose yet an additional surcharge on the 20 percent minority if higher revenue is needed to balance the budget, increase defense spending, or enlarge social programs. Congress would hardly want to incur the wrath of the 80 percent majority. Taxing everyone at the same rate does not invite the majority to gang up on a minority of taxpayers. It wouldn't take much to regain the current 50 percent rate.

Hall-Rabushka Versus Bradley-Gephardt

First, a scorecard on the Hall-Rabushka simple low flat tax.

1. All national income is taxed only once. Only investment spending and taxpayers' personal allowances are subtracted from national taxable income. No income is taxed twice. Except for compensation, all income is taxed at its business source, thus plugging leakage. By not allowing interest deductions for businesses and individuals, and not taxing interest receipts, the IRS would no longer reward borrowers at the expense of savers and consumers at the expense of investors. Spending financed by borrowed money would no longer be subsidized by the government. Savings and investment would no longer be taxed.

   The reason compensation income is taxed at the individual level is to insure that each tax filer gets the benefit of the personal allowance. It is important, too, that each taxpayer personally be aware of his tax contribution to government by filing an annual return. Otherwise, some might very well come to regard the government as a source of benefits without costs.

2. All income is taxed at the same *low* rate. The IRS would no longer punish successful people or those who receive dividend income (now double taxed into the 70 percent range). The tax system would no longer reward the clever tax avoiders, the sellers of shelters and legal advice, and those who incorporate to take advantage of retirement and other benefits. The IRS might even begin to collect taxes from people who sought refuge from high tax rates in the underground economy.

3. Households with incomes below the personal allowance pay no tax. The very poor are effectively shielded from having to pay income taxes.

4. All individuals and businesses could file their returns on a postcard (though in the interest of confidentiality we suggest they mail the postcard in an envelope). Admittedly, the paper industry stands to lose from true simplification of the tax code.

Now for the four-point scorecard on the Bradley-Gephardt stream-lined tax reform proposal.

1. Not all income is taxed even once, and considerable income is taxed twice. Since all but corporate profits are taxed at the level of the individual household, hundreds of billions of dollars of leakage remain unplugged. We see nothing in their plan changing people's behavior. Several hundred billions in six retained deductions further narrow the tax base. Because of the smaller tax base, surtaxes reaching 14 percent, added on top of a standard 14 percent rate, are required to match current collections.

   Taxation of corporate dividends in the hands of individuals constitutes double taxation. The same is true for interest receipts. First, taxes are paid on earnings. Then any savings from those earnings are again taxed when they earn interest. Some business income is even taxed three times: along with double taxation of corporate income and dividends is taxation of capital gains on stocks. Remember, higher stock prices reflect higher future earnings, which will be taxed when they occur.

   By retaining interest deductions, they still reward borrowers and consumers in direct proportion to marginal tax rates. Taxing interest penalizes savers and investors, also in proportion to marginal rates. Many people in the top surcharge bracket will still find interest-leveraged investment attractive, though shelters will be less attractive at 28 percent than the prior 50 percent rate.

2. The portion of national income that remains in the tax net is taxed at four different rates for individuals. The successful would still be punished. The effects of bracket-creep would be lessened, but not eliminated. Clever people would still shift income from high-bracket to low-bracket family members. Accountants and lawyers would still find advice-giving a lucrative enterprise.

3. The very poor would pay no income taxes.

4. Individuals would need almost as many schedules and pages of instructions as they now require. They would have to remain adroit at using their calculators. Many would still use commercial tax-preparers. Eliminating 26 deductions leaves most schedules intact or only slightly reduced. All 400 million 1099 statements of interest and dividend income would have to be

assembled. So too for millions of capital gains and losses transactions. Simpler? Yes. But really simple? Emphatically, no!

Finally, what about the effects on growth, interest rates, and new jobs? The Hall-Rabushka plan is, after all, a tax on consumption. By excluding all investment from taxable income, individuals and firms are encouraged to save and invest. We foresee an investment boom, a massive injection of badly needed capital into the American economy, rapid modernization of plant and equipment, and a sharp upturn in new venture capital for innovative firms. The results would be more jobs, higher-paying jobs, and rising after-tax real incomes. A low flat rate would not discourage overtime or harder work effort.

By contrast, Bradley-Gephardt continue to double tax a large amount of annual savings. They reward borrowers and consumers through interest deductions. By raising the capital gains tax rate, they discourage new equity investment. Levying higher real taxes on the most successful third of American taxpayers cannot induce greater work effort. At the first sign of fiscal crisis, Congress would be tempted to put further surcharges on the rich to raise more revenue. These are not growth-oriented incentives.

Admittedly, our plan raises taxes on a majority of Americans in its first year. But the economic benefits of higher growth soon overtake these first-year tax changes. In a short few years, a better-performing economy insures a more prosperous life for all. In contrast, Bradley-Gephardt promise small tax savings for 60 percent in their first year and higher taxes on the upper 30–40 percent. But the absence of growth incentives will not restore the economy. Stagnation and slow growth may continue, and the standard of living will slowly erode.

8 CHAPTER

Adopting the Flat Tax

All during 1982, the flat-tax bandwagon picked up a head of steam. As it became serious, critics charged that flat-tax advocates would run aground on the shoals of political realities. Vested interests would fight to preserve their special tax breaks. After all, they did not work so hard to get special tax treatment in the first place just to surrender those hard-won gains in the name of tax reform. Spokesmen for home builders, homeowners, savings and loans, charities, restaurants, and local governments, to name a few, have warned of dire repercussions from the repeal of tax-reducing privileges. When the opposition had marshalled its troops to counterattack, the flat-tax movement would go the way of all prior reform proposals.

We believe things are different today, that the time is ripe for true simplification of the tax system. The confluence of events that prompted the movement will not dissipate. Noncompliance, cheating, tax avoidance, and the underground economy are out of control. Burgeoning deficits, bracket creep, and new tax increase proposals promise further cuts in real purchasing power with no relief in sight. No one believes that fiscal responsibility can be restored in Washington. Nor will the economy reap the benefits of greater investment and productivity until high tax rates are sharply reduced.

The growing grass-roots movement for a flat-rate tax cuts across the entire social and political spectrum. The left, the right, and middle America have joined forces to secure a fair, simple, efficient tax system, to plug leaks and balance the federal budget. They see in the flat tax a progressive system that does not punish successful people with high marginal tax rates. They see the flat tax as an investment- oriented economic growth incentive.

It would be foolhardy to downplay the difficulties of enacting a true, simple flat-rate tax. But broad-based, grass-roots political movements in America have repeatedly overcome the resistance put up by congeries of special interests. Just four years ago in California the tax revolt was begun in earnest. Proposition 13 passed by a two-to-one majority, overcoming the concerted opposition of Governor Jerry Brown, the legislature, both political parties, private and public labor unions, major businesses, and the overwhelming majority of professors and intellectuals. The two-thirds majority was so broadly based that traditional social, economic, and political cleavages could not be discerned in the vote. Republican and Democrat, rich and poor, northerner and southerner, homeowner and renter, male and female, employed and unemployed, all voted for Proposition 13 in overwhelming numbers. The special interests were blown out of the water. All throughout 1982, the flat-tax movement enjoyed bipartisan support, in and out of Washington, D.C. We think preconditions are ripe for serious political appraisal of the flat tax.

Tax Subsidies

The federal government subsidizes many activities of businesses and individuals to reward or encourage specific types of behavior (e.g., home buying, energy exploration and conservation, local government bonds). It uses a variety of means to provide these subsidies: direct payments, credit subsidies, purchase guarantees, tax preferences, government regulations, trade policies, and government provision of private goods and services free or below cost. We are largely interested in the tax subsidies, since they would be directly affected by a simple flat tax.

In 1982, the Joint Committee on Taxation classified 109 separate provisions of the tax code as tax subsidy items. If all 109 items in the fiscal year 1983 budget were converted into direct spending outlays, their value would exceed $292 billion. Correspondingly, the revenue lost to the Treasury from granting these 109 functions preferential tax treatment is about $243 billion. But we already know that leakage severely contracts the tax base, forcing marginal rates to high levels.

Intuitively we know from reading our annual tax forms that tax breaks range over the full scale of economic life. The dozens of deductions and credits available on Form 1040, pages 1 and 2, Schedules A, C, and so on, reveal an enormous number of opportunities to reduce taxable income. The permissible areas include functions falling under national defense, international affairs, general science, space and technology, energy, natural resources and the environment, agriculture, commerce and housing credit, transportation, community and regional development, education, training, employment and social services, health, income security, veterans benefits and services, general government, general purpose fiscal assistance, and interest deferral on savings bonds. Not all 109 categories are equally important or powerful, but many would forcefully resist the loss of special status.

In some ways, the number 109 understates just how vast a stake in the existing tax code the special interests have. Take the deductibility of home mortgage interest, for example. The beneficiaries in this category include new home buyers, existing homeowners, holders of mortgages (the savings and loans), builders, bankers (who loan funds to builders), realtors, title companies, lawyers (who write purchase contracts), employees in all these businesses, and those who supply goods and services to these industries. Recipients of contributions likewise include many different kinds of activities ranging from churches and universities to museums and ballets.

We want to persuade you that our optimism over the flat tax is warranted. Our conviction does not lie in a naive belief that the government in Washington will do what is best for the majority of the people. American politics is a process of compromise, bargaining, and the attempt to win consent among varied, often conflicting elements in society on any given measure. Hundreds of interests vie with each other through explicit and implicit bargaining, in congressional committees, in the whole chambers of both houses of Congress, with the executive branch, and so on. The annual Directory of Washington Representatives lists thousands of groups and individuals registered to lobby the United States government. A select listing of Washington-based political action committees that spent more than $150,000 in 1981 includes the American Bankers Association, the American Dental Political Action Committee, the American Medical Political Action Committee, the Associated General Contractors Political Action Committee, the Attorneys Congressional Campaign Fund, the Build-Political Action Committee (of the National Association of Home Builders), the Business-Industry Political Action Committee, the Carpenters Legislative Improvement Committee, and we have only reached the letter C in the alphabet.

In addition to political action committees, equally large lists of business, economic, and regulation organizations exist to influence political outcomes. A few would include the Business Council, the Business Roundtable, the Chamber of Commerce of the United States, the National Association of Manufacturers, the American Savings and

Loan League, Inc., the National Savings and Loan League, the Institute for the Retention of Tax Exempt Municipal Bonds, the National Tax Limitation Committee, the National Taxpayers Union, and, to represent labor, the Truck Operations' Non-Partisan Committee, the Sheet Metal Workers' International Association Political Action League, and so forth.

In its May 22, 1982, issue, the *National Journal* highlighted tax lobbyists at work, trying to fight taxes that hit their clients. Author Timothy B. Clark enumerated Washington's top tax lobbyists, a who's who of highly-paid former Treasury Department employees, whose high-priced skills are widely sought to retain existing benefits, secure new benefits, or fight off potentially damaging changes. These lawyers and their firms orchestrate advertising, letter-writing and phone-calling campaigns to influence the media, public opinion, and members of Congress.

Millions of people stand to lose or gain billions of dollars every time the tax-writing committees of Congress sit down to work. Our flat tax would undo the entire current code. Virtually every person and organization in the entire country would feel the changes, and we think largely for the better. In the final pages of this book, we examine the most likely major opponents of a real flat tax along the lines of our plan. We hope to demonstrate that the momentum behind the flat tax can overcome the determined opposition.

The Special Interests

Let's start with American business in the most general sense. Our plan is singularly advantageous to the general conduct of business in the United States. We replace the hodgepodge of depreciation and investment tax credits, both general and specific, with 100 percent writeoff of all investment in its first year. This substitution makes investment even more attractive as it simultaneously simplifies current bookkeeping. Equally important, we lower the tax rate on business income from 46 percent for corporations and up to 50 percent for unincorporated business to a low standard charge of 19 percent. With unlimited carry-forward of tax losses, we cut taxes on young, innovative, rapidly growing firms, like Apple Computer, and raise taxes on established, high-earning companies, like Exxon. Our plan is a tax on consumption. Money invested in the economy is not taxed; thus investment is encouraged. Money withdrawn and consumed is taxed.

Economists agree that a low flat-rate tax on consumption is very conducive to high rates of work effort and economic growth.

What would happen to such current business expenses as travel, three-martini lunches, season tickets to entertain clients watching the St. Louis Cardinals play baseball (winning, we hope), club memberships, and so on? And what about perks? Nothing would change for ordinary business expenses, except the incentives. But fringe benefits would now be taxed and not wastefully increased in lieu of compensation solely to the tax benefit of employees. With a current corporate profits tax at 46 percent, a firm can provide its employees with highly subsidized benefits. Under our plan, the subsidy element in expenses falls from 46 cents to 19 cents on the dollar, and disappears altogether for fringes. When you take a potential business client to lunch and deduct the cost as a normal business expense, the savings in taxes is only 19 cents on the dollar, compared with the current 46 cents. Stockholders will find a steady return at 81 cents for each earned dollar a strong incentive to curtail wasteful business practices. We would expect business managers to watch their expenses more closely in a 19 percent world. As a people, we are used to thinking in a 50 percent world and will find our thinking much different in a 19 percent world. You can imagine the hundreds of ways you would arrange your financial affairs differently.

In its broadest dimensions, then, American business will gain from the Hall-Rabushka flat tax. It maximizes investment incentives, minimizes explicit tax rates, and enhances the environment for profitable entrepreneurial, risk-taking behavior. By eliminating the tax on capital gains from the buying and selling of stocks and securities, money will flow into investment opportunities.

We think our package of low tax rates and improved incentives for businesses more than offsets the loss of deductibility of excise and property taxes, preferential treatment for corporate pensions, taxation of fringes, and the loss of interest deductions. With interest receipts placed on an after-tax basis, people would be encouraged to put their money in interest-earning assets.

We expect, therefore, considerable support from the major American business organizations. We would hope to attract the efforts of the Business Council, the Business Roundtable, the Chamber of Commerce of the United States, the Conference Board, the Council for a Competitive Economy, the National Association of Manufacturers, the American Council on Capital Formation, and others to write, speak, and work for a plan like ours. We would expect these organizations and their members to share our expectation that a flat tax would stem the erosion in capital formation and business profits, restoring productivity and profitability.

There remain some business activities that receive narrowly defined tax benefits. Examples include conservation and new technology credits, research and development credits, and energy exploration. However, in exchange for giving up special concessions, these businesses would benefit from low tax rates, full investment writeoff, untaxed capital gains on their securities, the elimination of double taxation, simplified tax forms, and, most important, much harder-working employees, who would no longer face the disincentive of 50 percent marginal tax rates.

So far, so good. A consumption tax by its nature is a tax that encourages the investment needed to produce goods and services. What about the rest of the population? In particular, how will other beneficiaries of tax subsidies evaluate the flat tax, especially those who benefit from the tax subsidies in the areas of housing, consumer credit, health care, state and local governments, pensions, workmen's compensation, unemployment insurance benefits, and the armed forces.

Interest payments are the most widely used deduction by individuals. For fiscal year 1983, the value of interest deductions expressed in what government would have to spend to provide comparable benefits is $25.8 billion for home mortgage, $9.3 billion for consumer credit, $1 billion for the interest exclusion from state and local pollution control bonds, $2.3 billion for state and local industrial development bonds, $7.7 billion for general purpose state and local government debt, $1.3 billion for state and local government bonds used to finance owner-occupied housing, and $6.8 billion for life insurance savings. $50 billion is no small sum.

Consider the loss of the mortgage interest deduction. Recall in Chapter 4 our treatment of this major controversy. Recent home buyers and those with an old mortgage would fare no worse. The benefit of lower interest rates that would follow adoption of our plan would approximately equal the loss in interest deduction. Builders of new homes and realtors would be no worse off. Holders of existing mortgages—the financially hard-pressed savings and loans—would gain from the increased value of their mortgages as interest rates fell. Those homeowners who bought in the mid- to late seventies would suffer the most, but even their situation would ultimately improve as a better-performing economy increased overall demand for housing a few years hence. Since most homeowners face marginal rates above 19 percent, they would also benefit from lower marginal rates. From this perspective, the presumed housing lobby does not present so formidable a political obstacle.

Putting interest on an after-tax basis terminates the advantages of tax exemptions and lower interest rates currently enjoyed by state and local government bonds. Under our plan, local governments would no longer be able to borrow at lower rates than, say, corporations. State and local governments would have to compete on even terms with private borrowers for the public's money. Since interest rates will fall in the entire economy, borrowing costs would not rise for local governments.

What benefits would state and local governments get? Mainly a healthier economy, with productive businesses and individuals earning more and, over the long run, paying more taxes into state and local government treasuries. High unemployment and economic stagnation are a chief source of fiscal difficulty in state capitals and city halls. Vigorous economic growth would offset the benefits that state and local governments enjoy not only from tax-exempt bonds, but also from deducting all nonbusiness state, local, and property taxes. A return to healthy economic growth is more than a fair price to pay for the temporary problems our plan inflicts on local governments.

Apart from home mortgage interest, the second most controversial effect of a flat tax is on tax-deductible contributions to a wide variety of purposes. Again, turn back to Chapter 4. We estimated that at most 10 percent of contributions would decline, assuming those with tax cuts did not pick up any of the slack. But some will surely be made up. We think churches will receive more contributions. On the other hand, elitist institutions may fare worse, but they can charge their affluent consumers higher fees to compensate or perhaps should be allowed to go out of business. After all, it seems wholly inappropriate to use the tax code just to keep an organization or activity solvent if the merit of its activities could not attract sufficient funds. We doubt that any charity serving the truly needy would be forced to shut down.

Turning to other tax subsidies, our plan also eliminates the current child care deduction (which Bradley-Gephardt proposes to convert to a credit). One reason for child care deductions is to reduce the marriage penalty two-earner families would otherwise have to pay for child care from after tax income, already taxed at high marginal rates due to their combined earnings. A 19 percent flat tax eliminates the marriage penalty, thus compensating two-earner families in lower marginal rates for the loss of deducting child care costs.

The alert reader will have noticed that we have touched on virtually all the major deductions retained in Bradley-Gephardt, we presume, for their political attractiveness. Most of the other tax preferences disappear in their plan as well as ours. We suspect they examined the political landscape and gave up further potential broadening of the tax base in exchange for political appeal to the numerous and vocal interests represented in the major deductions and credits they keep. Their plan and ours eliminates the special tax benefits accorded armed forces personnel, residential energy, conservation and new technology, workman's compensation, casualty losses, medical costs (not over 10 percent of AGI for Bradley-Gephardt), and others. We jointly perceive that the organizations and interests that benefit in these categories do not seriously threaten the political feasibility of broadening the tax base and cutting tax rates.

As you think about the political prospects of the flat tax, it is worthwhile to keep your bookmark firmly in place in Chapter 6. There we answer dozens of questions about how our plan will affect you, your job or business, and different industries and professions. Our questions and answers address all the major areas of our economy that will be affected by switching to the simple flat tax. In most cases, an assumed loss of benefits fails to materialize or is minor at worst. In cases of visible loss, offsetting gains are provided in the form of lower tax rates. Finally, for those few who still face real losses, higher growth rates for the economy promise to increase their real after-tax income in the near future, leaving everyone better off from the incentive effects of the flat tax.

Why then has there been such a hue and cry that the flat tax has no chance of passage? First, public outrage over the federal income tax is relatively recent. Other issues held center stage. Now public support for a flat-tax reform collectively exceeds all of the individual sentiments to preserve one or more tax breaks added together. 1982 marked the first year in modern history that members of the Democratic Party opened and led the drive for a tax reform to improve incentives.

Second, until 1982, the flat tax was only a good idea. Now our plan and others offer a comprehensive alternative to the entire current corporate and individual income tax code. Tax reform requires a viable alternative—you can't beat somebody with nobody. With the development of a detailed plan, the forces seeking a truly simple flat tax have a concrete piece of legislation around which they can unite.

Third, tax reform plans in prior years threatened to eliminate current benefits, without stopping up leakage, treating all business income consistently, or compensating those who stand to lose deductions with much lower marginal rates. Our plan is also much more likely to balance the federal budget than the current system or the plans others have put forth in prior years.

Finally, intellectuals and liberal politicians have always said that high marginal tax rates were inherent to any progressive system. But the dismal performance of the economy since 1975 has jolted their thinking: even Joe Pechman of the Brookings Institution favors lowering all marginal rates. There is even a growing consensus that graduated rates are not essential to progressivity. It would have been nearly impossible just two or three years ago to gain endorsement of the flat tax from such people as Ralph Nader. With the turning of the intellectual tide, we expect the political tide to turn as well.

A Flat-Tax Law

Subtitle A of the Internal Revenue Code of 1954, ''Income Taxes,'' is repealed and replaced with the following:

Contents

Chapter 1. Computation of taxable income

Section 1. Compensation defined

Compensation means all cash amounts paid by an employer or received by an employee, including wages, salaries, pensions, bonuses, prizes, and awards. Compensation includes:

(a) the value of any financial instrument conveyed to an employee, measured as market value at the time of conveyance;

(b) Workman's Compensation and other payments for injuries or other compensation for damages.

Compensation excludes:

(a) reimbursements to employees by employers for business expenses paid by the taxpayer in connection with performance by him or her of services as an employee;

(b) goods and services provided to employees by employers, including but not limited to medical benefits, insurance, meals, housing, recreational facilities, and other fringe benefits;

(c) wages, salaries, and other payments for services performed outside the United States.

119

Section 2. Business receipts defined

Business receipts are the cash receipts of a business from the sale of products or services produced in or passing through the United States. Business receipts include:

(a) gross revenue, including sales and excise taxes, from the sale of goods and services;

(b) fees, commissions and similar receipts, if not reported as compensation;

(c) gross rents;

(d) royalties;

(e) gross receipts from the sale of plant, equipment, and land;

(f) the market value of goods, services, plant, equipment, or land provided to its owners or employees;

(g) the market value of goods, services, and equipment delivered from the United States to points outside the United States, if not included in sales;

(h) the market value of goods and services provided to depositors, insurance policyholders, and others with a financial claim upon the business, if not included in sales.

Section 3. Cost of business inputs defined

The cost of business inputs is the actual cost of purchases of goods, services, and materials required for business purposes. The cost of business inputs includes:

(a) the actual amount paid for goods, services, and materials, whether or not resold during the year;

(b) the market value of business inputs brought into the United States;

(c) the actual cost, if reasonable, of travel and entertainment expenses for business purposes.

The cost of business inputs excludes purchases of goods and services provided to employees or owners, unless these are included in business receipts.

Section 4. Cost of capital equipment, structures, and land defined

The cost of capital equipment, structures, and land includes any purchases of these items for business purposes. In the case of equipment brought into the United States, the cost is the market value at time of entry into the United States.

Section 5. Business taxable income defined

Business taxable income is business receipts less the cost of business inputs, less compensation paid to employees, and less the cost of capital equipment, structures, and land.

Chapter 2. Determination of tax liability

Section 1. Personal allowances

For the year 1982, personal allowances are:

(a) For married taxpayers filing jointly, $6200. A taxpayer is considered married if he was married at the end of the year or his spouse died during the year.

(b) For heads of households, $5600. A taxpayer is a head of a household if he is not married, and maintains as his home a household which is the principal home of a dependent son, stepson, daughter, stepdaughter, mother, or father of the taxpayer, and the taxpayer provides more than half the support for the dependent.

(c) For single taxpayers, $3800.

(d) For each dependent, $750. A dependent is a son, stepson, daughter, stepdaughter, mother, or father of the taxpayer, for whom the taxpayer provides more than half support.

Each year, personal allowances rise by the proportional increase from the beginning to the end of the immediately preceding year in the Consumer Price Index of the Department of Commerce.

Section 2. Compensation tax

Each individual employed at any time during the year will pay a tax of 19 percent of his compensation less his personal allowance, or no tax if his compensation is less than his personal allowance.

Section 3. Business tax

(a) Business defined

Each sole proprietorship, partnership, and corporation constitutes a business. Any organization or individual not specifically exempt under Chapter 3, with business receipts, is a business.

(b) Computation of tax

Each business will pay a tax of 19 percent of its business taxable income, or zero if business taxable income is negative.

(c) Filing units

A business may file any number of business tax returns for its various subsidiaries or other units, provided that all business receipts are reported in the aggregate, and provided that each expenditure for business inputs is reported on no more than one return.

(d) Carry-forward of losses

When business taxable income is negative, the negative amount may be used to offset positive taxes in future years. The amount carried forward from one year to the next is augmented according to an interest rate equal to the average daily yield on three-month Treasury Bills during the first year. There is no limit to the amount or the duration of the carry-forward.

Chapter 3. Exempt organizations.

Organizations exempt from the business tax are:

(a) state and local governments, and their subsidiary units;

(b) educational, religious, charitable, philanthropic, cultural, and community service organizations that do not return income to individual or corporate owners.

Chapter 4. Withholding

Each employer, including exempt organizations, will withhold from the wages, salaries, and pensions of its employees, and remit to the Internal Revenue Service, an amount computed as follows: 19 percent of the excess of compensation in each pay period over the employee's annual personal allowance, pro-rated for the length of the pay period.

The Tax Base

Following are the relevant numbers from the U.S. National Income and Product Accounts for 1981. All data are in billions of current dollars.

Gross domestic product[1]	$2868
Federal indirect business tax[2]	57
Imputed items[3]	129
Wages, salaries, and pensions[4]	1503
Investment[5]	349
Taxable business income[6]	830
Revenue from the business tax at 19%	158
Taxable compensation[7]	1022
Revenue from compensation tax at 19%	194
Total tax revenue	352
Actual personal income tax[8]	289
Actual corporate income tax[9]	57
Total actual tax revenue	348

Notes:

[1] *Economic Report of the President*, January 1982, Table B–8.

[2] *ERP*, Table B–76.

[3] *Survey of Current Business*, "National Income and Product Accounts, 1976–1979," Special Supplement, July 1981, Table 8.8, p. 77.

[4] *ERP*, Table B–21 plus our estimate of private pensions.

[5] Business investment is estimated as total investment in equipment, nonresidential structures, and farm investment, plus 20 percent of investment in residential structures, *ERP*, Table B–15. The remaining 80 percent of residential structures are owner-occupied and not deductible under the business tax.

[6] Gross domestic product less federal indirect business taxes, wages, salaries and pensions, imputed items, and investment.

[7] Wages, salaries, and pensions less personal allowances.

[8] Estimated as 75 percent of the revenue for fiscal year 1981 and 25 percent of the revenue for fiscal year 1982, *ERP*, Table B–19.

[9] Same as personal income tax.

C APPENDIX

Tax Burden by Income Groups

Our goal is to compute the tax paid on the total income received by families and individuals in various income groups. We do this first for the existing personal and corporate taxes, and then for the simple flat tax. All the data come from Internal Revenue Service tabulations of income tax returns and from the National Income and Product Accounts.

The first step is to approximate the income omitted from Adjusted Gross Income in the IRS data. The first component is fringe benefits. In the NIPA for 1979, total fringes are $225 billion. Wage income reported in tax returns was $1229 billion, almost exactly the same as the $1236 in the NIPA. We assume that fringes in each AGI category are in proportion to wage and salary income in that category, in the proportion 225/1229, or $0.183 in fringes for each $1.00 in wages and salaries. The second component of unreported income is that associated with business ownership, broadly construed. We assume that leakage other than fringe benefits is in proportion to business income in each AGI category. The base of the simple tax was $1926 billion in 1979, while the total AGI was $1465, so total leakage was $461 billion. Of this, $225 has already been accounted as fringes. The remainder, $236 billion, is corporate retained earnings and other components of business income not reported as AGI. We assume that extra business income in each AGI category is in proportion to reported dividends in that category, in the proportion 236/35, or $6.74 in unreported business income for each $1.00 in reported dividends. Total reported dividends were $35 billion.

The second step is to compute taxes paid under the existing personal and corporate taxes. Personal income taxes are reported directly by the IRS by AGI category. We assume that corporate taxes in each AGI category are in proportion to dividends in that category, in the proportion 65/35, or $1.86 in corporate tax per $1.00 in dividends. Total corporate taxes in 1979 were $65 billion.

The third step is to compute taxes under the simple flat tax. This requires computing the personal allowances by AGI category. The IRS reports the fraction of taxpayers married and the number of dependents per taxpayer by AGI category. We estimated the fraction of taxpayers who were heads of households as the number of dependents per taxpayer divided by 1.45, less the fraction married. We computed the fraction of taxpayers who were single

124

by subtracting the fraction married and the fraction who were heads of households from one. Then we computed the average personal allowance in each income category as $4500 times the fraction married plus $4050 times the fraction who were heads of households plus $2700 times the fraction single plus $540 times the average number of dependents. These figures deflate our 1982 personal allowances to 1979 levels. Finally, we computed the simple tax as 19 percent of the difference between augmented income and the average personal allowance.

Following are the results of the computations:

Augmented income	Current tax	Simple tax	Change as a % of income
$ 5,687	$ 247	$ 440	3.4%
9,232	574	1,059	5.2
11,635	905	1,494	5.1
14,099	1,250	1,919	4.7
17,629	1,726	2,535	4.6
21,244	2,246	3,166	4.3
27,663	3,260	4,318	3.8
33,505	4,286	5,404	3.3
44,196	6,532	7,417	2.0
58,753	10,333	10,182	− 0.3
88,750	18,640	15,879	− 3.1
135,079	34,191	24,681	− 7.0
251,870	67,973	46,870	− 8.4
691,239	202,384	130,382	− 10.4
1,792,476	577,080	339,652	− 13.2

Sources:

Internal Revenue Service, *Statistics of Income—1979, Individual Income Tax Returns*, Washington, D.C., 1982.

Economic Report of the President, February 1982, Appendix B, Statistical Tables Relating to Income, Employment, and Production.

Future Deficits

TABLE 1 presents our computations based on the economic assumptions and spending proposals in the president's February 1982 budget.

TABLE 1					
	81	82	83	84	85
GNP	$2,922	$3,159	$3,522	$3,881	$4,257
Tax base	2,314	2,502	2,789	3,074	3,372
Allowances	481	535	580	620	655
Taxable income	1,833	1,967	2,210	2,454	2,717
Taxable inc., fiscal year	1,790	1,933	2,149	2,393	2,651
Revenue, personal and corporate inc. taxes	347	345	370	407	450
Rate to raise same revenue	19.4	17.8	17.2	17.0	17.0
Rate to close deficit			21.2	20.0	19.0
Revenue at 19% tax rate			408	455	504
Deficit at 19% tax rate	58	99	51	29	8

The first four lines compute the level of taxable income on a calendar-year basis. The fifth line gives taxable income on a fiscal year basis. When divided into an estimate of required revenue, taxable income gives the necessary tax rate under the simple tax.

The next line, labeled "Revenue, personal and corporate inc. taxes," gives the administration's estimates of the revenue from the personal and corporate income taxes, including the effects of ERTA and the modifications proposed by the president in February. The line below, labeled "Rate to raise same revenue" gives the rate under the simple tax necessary to yield the same revenue as the personal and corporate income taxes. Note that the rate declines from around 19 percent in 1981 to 17 percent in later years, as the major personal tax reductions of 1982 and 1983 go into effect.

The next line, labeled "Rate to close deficit," gives the simple tax rate necessary to eliminate the deficit starting in FY 1983. Though this rate starts above 21 percent, it falls to 19 percent by 1985. Again, these computations take account of the favorable effect on interest costs of lower deficits in earlier years.

The last line shows the projected size of the federal deficit if the simple tax were adopted starting in FY 83 at a constant rate of 19 percent. The deficit is manageable in all years and essentially disappears in 1985.

TABLE 2 presents similar computations for the CBO's baseline budget projections.

TABLE 2							
	81	82	83	84	85	86	87
GNP	$2922	$3140	$3515	$3882	$4259	$4659	$5083
Tax base	2314	2487	2784	3075	3373	3690	4026
Allowances	481	535	581	627	676	726	777
Taxable income	1833	1952	2203	2448	2697	2964	3249
Taxable income, fiscal year	1790	1922	2140	2387	2635	2897	3178
Revenue, personal and corporate taxes	347	350	354	378	407	431	469
Rate to raise same revenue	19.4	18.2	16.5	15.8	15.4	14.9	14.8
Rate to close deficit			23.4	22.5	21.7	20.9	20.2
Deficit at 19% rate			101	102	97	87	75

The format of this table is the same as that of Table 1, except that it covers two additional years. The administration and the CBO are projecting GNP at about the same level through 1985, though the administration foresees higher levels of real growth and lower rates of inflation.

Allowances grow more rapidly under the CBO projection as a consequence.

The simple tax rates necessary to raise the same revenue as the personal and corporate income taxes fall to even lower levels—below 15 percent—under the CBO's assumptions, because the administration's revenue enhancements are not included in the baseline. On the other hand, the tax rate necessary to balance the budget starting in FY 83, shown in the next-to-last line in the table, is about a point higher because the CBO projects significantly higher federal spending than does the administration.

The last line of Table 2 shows that with higher spending and weaker real growth, the simple tax at a fixed rate of 19 percent does not eliminate the federal deficit even by 1987. However, it does bring it well below $100 billion, as against the CBO's projection of nearly $250 billion.

Sources:

Budget of the United States Government, Fiscal Year 1983, February 1982.

Congressional Budget Office, *Baseline Budget Projections for Fiscal Years 1983–1987, A Report to the Senate and House Committees on the Budget—Part II*, February 1982.

Notes and References

Chapter 1: Why the Income Tax Has Failed

The literature on the federal income tax is enormous. A good up-to-date summary is contained in Harold L. Wattel (ed.), *The Gross Personal Income Tax*, Hofstra University Yearbook of Business, Series 17, Volume 1, 1982. The essays contained in this yearbook weigh the pros and cons of switching from a graduated income tax to a flat-rate tax.

The complexity of the income tax is best seen in the *United States Code of Federal Regulations, Title 26*, updated by the Economic Recovery Tax Act of 1981 and the Tax Equity and Fiscal Responsibility Act of 1982. Specific assertions of the system's excessive complexity are also found in reports of the General Accounting Office. *Who's Not Filing Income Tax Returns? IRS Needs Better Ways to Find Them and Collect Their Taxes*, Publication GGD-79-69, July 11, 1979, and *What IRS Can Do to Collect More Delinquent Taxes*, Publication GGD-82-4, November 5, 1981.

Information and estimates on the paperwork and direct dollar costs of filing annual tax returns appear in the *Annual Reports* of the Commissioner of Internal Revenue, in *A Report of the Commission on Federal Paperwork: Taxation*, June 10, 1978, and *Paperwork and Red Tape: - New Perspectives, - New Directions;* A Report to the President and Congress from the Office of Management and Budget, June 1978.

Two general all-purpose references for calculating the size and growth of government taxes and spending are the *Economic Report of the President*, published each January, and the monthly *Treasury Bulletin*, published by the Treasury Department, showing receipts and outlays monthly with annual totals reaching back ten years.

The literature on tax avoidance and evasion is mushrooming. To determine the extent of avoidance, we recommend careful examination of the annual Internal Revenue Service publication titled *Statistics of Income, Individual Income Tax Returns*. It lists the value of every deduction taxpayers declare on their returns by category. The total aggregate value of all tax subsidy items in the economy are enumerated by category in *Special Analysis G. Tax Expenditures. The Budget of the United States Government, 1983*, Office of Management and Budget, Executive Office of the President, February 1982.

Official and unofficial estimates exist on the extent of growing tax evasion. Official estimates include *Estimates of Income Unreported on Individual Tax Returns*, Department of the Treasury, Internal Revenue Service, Publication 1104 (9–79). Academic and popular accounts are contained in Vito Tanzi (ed.), *The Underground Economy in the United States and Abroad,* Lexington, Massachusetts: D. C. Heath, 1982; Dan Bawly, *The Subterranean Economy,* New York: McGraw-Hill, 1982; Carl P. Simon and Ann D. Witte, *Beating the System: The Underground Economy,* Boston: Auburn House, 1982; and "The Underground Economy's Hidden Force," *Business Week,* April 5, 1982, pp. 64–70.

For those readers who want a lucid exposition of the philosophy and evidence underlying supply-side economics, we recommend Bruce Bartlett, *Reaganomics: Supply-Side Economics in Action,* Westport, Conn.: Arlington House, 1981; George Gilder, *Wealth and Poverty,* New York: Basic Books, 1981; and Jude Wanniski, *The Way the World Works,* New York: Basic Books, 1978. While we do not necessarily agree with any or all of the views of these authors, they represent the most explicit, readable statements on supply-side economics. More rigorous treatments of the subject can be found in David G. Raboy (ed.), *Essays in Supply-Side Economics,* Washington, D.C.: Institute for Research on the Economics of Taxation, 1982.

Chapter 2: The Flat-Tax Movement

Milton Friedman's proposal for a flat-rate income tax was presented in *Capitalism and Freedom,* Chicago: University of Chicago Press, 1962. Somewhat more recent are the proceedings of a debate held by the American Enterprise Institute in 1969. In published form it is Charles O. Galvin and Boris I. Bittker, *The Income Tax: How Progressive Should It Be?* Washington, D.C.: American Enterprise Institute, 1969. In that debate, Galvin makes the case for a low-rate, broad-based income tax system. Of more recent vintage is the Treasury Department report conducted during the administration of former Secretary William E. Simon, known as *Blueprints for Basic Tax Reform,* 1977. In a 1981 pamphlet also published by the American Enterprise Institute entitled *Reforming the Income Tax System,* William Simon makes the case for broadening the tax base and lowering marginal rates.

A good example of the recency of the intellectual transformation in favor of the flat tax is seen in a Brookings Institution conference held in December 1976, published in 1977. Forty-four participants from universities, the Treasury, the Congress, tax law firms, and international financial bodies discussed such issues as personal deductions, employee benefits and transfer payments, capital gains and losses, homeowner tax preferences, treatment of the family, the definition of taxable business income, and other topics. Only one of the 44 participants advocated a proportional flat-rate tax. See Joseph Pechman (ed.), *Comprehensive Income Taxation,* Washington, D.C.: Brookings Institution, 1977. On page 271 is the following statement: "One solution to the conflict of objectives would be to replace the progressive rate schedules with a proportional rate. A per capita allowance—either a deduction or a tax credit—would provide some degree of progressivity in average tax rates. One conference participant advocated this solution, *but his suggestion was ignored,* presumably because it would sacrifice too much of the progressivity of the income tax, particularly at higher income levels.'' [emphasis added] The times have definitely changed.

Three outstanding treatments describing and explaining the effects of Great Britain's flat-rate income tax during the late nineteenth century are Stephen Dowell, *A History of Taxation and Taxes in England,* Vol. II, London: Longmans, Green, and Co., 1888; Sydney Buxton, *Finance and Politics: An Historical Study. 1783–1885,* Vols. 1 and 2, London, John Murray, 1888; and John Noble, *National Finance: A Review of the Policy of the Last Two Parliaments, and of the Results of Modern Fiscal Legislation,* London: Longmans, Green and Co., 1875. For a detailed account of William E. Gladstone as Chancellor of the Exchequer and Prime Minister, see Francis W. Hirst, *Gladstone as Financier and Economist,* London: Ernest Benn Limited, 1931.

For a comprehensive discussion of Hong Kong's tax system and its effect on the performance of the Hong Kong economy, see two books by Alvin Rabushka. One is entitled *Value for Money: The Hong Kong Budgetary Process,* Stanford: Hoover Press, 1976, and the other *Hong Kong: A Study in Economic Freedom,* Chicago: University of Chicago Press, 1979. A detailed local Hong Kong publication is that of Peter Willoughby, *Hong Kong Taxation, A Miscellany,* published by the South China Morning Post, 1977.

Chapter 3: A Practical, Low, Simple, Flat Tax

The data on fringe benefits as a fraction of total compensation are in Table B-21 of the Statistical Tables Relation to Income, Employment, and Production, *Economic Report of the President, 1982.*

Operating data for the Exxon Corporation, Apple Computer, and the Old National Bank came from their corporate annual reports for 1981. All the other returns are completely fictitious.

For the details on the taxes and subsidies in the current taxation of capital, see Charles R. Hulten (ed.) *Depreciation, Inflation, and the Taxation of Income from Capital,* Urban Institute Press, Washington, 1981.

Data on the market value of the services of banks, currently deducted from interest, see the *Survey of Current Business,* Special Supplement, July 1981.

Chapter 4: The Big Economic Issues

Data on tax rates by income categories appear in Internal Revenue Service, *Statistics of Income—1979, Individual Income Tax Returns,* Washington, D.C., 1982, Table 3.13, p. 97.

The study by Jerry Hausman is in Henry J. Aaron and Joseph A. Pechman (eds.), *How Taxes Affect Economic Behavior,* Brookings Institution, Washington, D.C., 1981, pp. 27–84.

The data on output per hour of work are from Table B-40, Statistical Tables Relating to Income, Employment, and Production, *Economic Report of the President, 1982.*

Data on charitable contributions are from the American Association of Fund-Raising Counsel, Inc., *Giving USA,* 1980, for the data on 1979, and 1982, for the value of contributed time.

Chapter 5: Transition to the Flat Tax

Data on depreciation and interest deductions come from Internal Revenue Service, *Statistics of Income—1979, Individual Income Tax Returns and Partnership Returns,* and *Statistics of Income—1978–1979, Corporation Income Tax Returns.*

Index

OTHER BOOKS BY ROBERT E. HALL

Inflation: Causes and Effects. University of Chicago Press for the National Bureau of Economic Research, 1982. (Editor)

OTHER BOOKS BY ALVIN RABUSHKA

Politics in Plural Societies: A Theory of Democratic Instability. Charles E. Merrill, 1972. (Co-author)

Race and Politics in Urban Malaya. Hoover Institution Press, 1973.

The Changing Face of Hong Kong. American Enterprise Institute, 1973.

A Theory of Racial Harmony. University of South Carolina Press, 1974.

The Urban Elderly Poor: Racial and Bureaucratic Conflict. Lexington Books, 1974. (Co-author)

Value for Money: The Hong Kong Budgetary Process. Hoover Institution Press, 1976.

Caseworkers or Police? How Tenants See Public Housing. Hoover Institution Press, 1977. (Co-author)

Hong Kong: A Study in Economic Freedom. University of Chicago Press, 1979.

Old Folks at Home. Free Press, 1980. (Co-author)

The United States in the 1980s. Hoover Institution Press, 1980. (Co-editor)

The Tax Revolt. Hoover Institution Press, 1982. (Co-author)